Supplementary Workbook for
A New Text for a Modern China

Shining Zou and Feng Lan

Cheng & Tsui Company

First Printing 2001

Cheng and Tsui Company
25 West Street
Boston, MA 02111-1213 USA
Fax: (617) 426-3669
www.cheng-tsui.com

ISBN 0887273939

The textbook, *A New Text for a Modern China,* and accompanying audio tapes are also available from the publisher.

Printed in Canada

INTRODUCTION

This *WORKBOOK* provides supplementary exercises for the textbook *A NEW TEXT FOR A MODERN CHINA*. It was field-tested in the Chinese School of the East Asian Summer Language Institute at Indiana University (EASLI) during the summers of 1997, 1998, and 1999, and at the Florida State University in the fall of 1999. In designing the workbook, the authors have followed the pedagogical premises of the original textbook to help students master the major Chinese vocabulary, idiomatic expressions and sentence patterns found in the textbook, and to help them further explore the socio-cultural issues on which the textbook focuses. The workbook consists of nineteen sections in correspondence to the nineteen lessons of the original textbook. Each section presents in both simplified and traditional characters a variety of exercises serving different purposes. Teachers may assign the exercises that best suit the needs of their students. These exercises fall into four categories.

1. **Vocabulary exercises** stress the proper understanding of new vocabulary items, a solid grasp of frequently-used polyphonic characters, adequate word collocations, and the correct use of adjectives and attributive phrases.
    Examples:
    A · 划线组词
    (Construct phrases by paring related words with a line.)
    B · 写出反义词
    (Write down the antonyms of the words.)
    C · 组成动宾词组
    (Construct verb-object phrases.)
    D · 给句中划线的词注音，并仿造例句造句
    (Give the pinyin of the underlined words and make sentences following the examples.)
    E · 选词填空
    (Fill in the blanks with adequate words.)
    F · 用汉语解释下列词语
    (Explain the meanings of the words below in Chinese.)

2. **Syntax and grammar exercises** help students use correct sentence patterns as well as proper common words and expressions in a sentence or passage.
    Examples:
    A · 完成句子
    (Complete the sentences.)
    B · 仿照例句，用所给的句式完成句子

(Following the examples, complete the sentences with the given sentence patterns or words.)

    C · 用指定的词改写句子

    (Rewrite the sentences by using the given words.)

    D · 看图造句或回答问题

    (Make sentences or answer the questions based on the pictures.)

    E · 用所给词语将英语句子译成中文

    (Translate the English sentences into Chinese by using the given words or phrases.)

3. **Reading comprehension and composition** help students understand related supplementary reading materials and allow them to fully utilize in writing the vocabulary and sentence structures obtained from studying the main text of the lesson.

    Examples:

        A · 读短文，选择正确的答案

        (Read the short passage and choose the correct answers.)

        B · 读副课文，回答问题

        (Read the supplementary text and answer the questions.)

        C · 写文章

        (Composition.)

4. **Reflections on and discussions of social issues** give students the chances to discuss related social issues in an in-depth and broad way, and enable them to learn to verbalize their individual opinions correctly and intelligently.

    Examples:

        A · 想一想，说一说

        (Think and talk.)

We are indebted to Professor Jen-mei Ma for her invaluable suggestions and advice related to the manuscript. We are also deeply grateful to Professor Irene Liu for her support in the publication of this workbook.

TABLE OF CONTENTS

目录

1 · 人口　　住房

一、用所给的字组词：

例：急---急迫

提---　　　　　　　　　　　　生---

增---　　　　　　　　　　　　失---

收---　　　　　　　　　　　　报---

交---　　　　　　　　　　　　居---

二、划线，组成动宾词组：

增长　　　　　　　　　　　　影响

提高　　　　　　　　　　　　政策

提出　　　　　　　　　　　　水平

解决　　　　　　　　　　　　收入

带来　　　　　　　　　　　　问题

三、选词填空：

以前......以后　　　　　　　以前......后来

1·_____他整天玩，不学习，考试成绩很不好。今天他下决心，____
再也不贪玩了。

2·_____他常常开快车，_____出事故了，弄得车毁人伤，他就再也
不敢开快车了。

3·_____我们是好朋友，他去了中国_____，我们就失去了联系。

4・_____中国的出生率很高，人口增长得很快，_____政府推行了计划生育的政策，使人口的增长得到了控制。

       平均   平衡

1・在那个地区，人们一年的_____收入是两千美元。

2・你的饮食结构要_____，既要吃菜，又要吃肉。

3・这个企业今年收支不_____，要亏本了。

4・你这个学期的_____成绩是多少分？

       才   就

1・我都等了你二十分钟了，你_____来呀。

2・我五点_____来了，一直在等你。

3・他读了三遍那个故事，我_____听懂。

4・她一个人_____有三套房子。

四、用所给的词，完成句子：

1・虽然他没去过中国，_____。（可是）

2・要学好中文，就要_____。（不断）

3・他让我上课别迟到，_____。（却）

4・我们刚刚做了一个听写测验，_____。（跟着）

5・我不喜欢他，_____。（因为）

6・这道题他讲了五遍，_____。（还是）

五、造句：

1・可是

2

2 · 太

3 · 跟

4 · 比如

5 · 影响

六、用所给词语将下列句子译成中文：

1. There are two reports in today's newspaper. The first one concerns the problem of unemployment in the United States; the second one deals with the problem of transportation. （谈的是）

2. Chinese is an important language because one out of five people in the world speaks this language. （平均......中）

3. China is confronted with many serious social issues, such as population, housing, corruption, and so on. （比如......等等）

4. The number of students at this university has doubled within three years. （增长）

5. Five years ago, he made only $25,000 a year. Now his annual income has already exceeded $80,000. （超过）

6. The rapid increase in population has created an enormous impact on the living standard of the Chinese people. （带来）

7. Although the government introduced a special policy to help the poor as early as the late 1970s, poverty still remains a serious social problem in this country. （提出......政策）

8. Presently the shortage of housing is a pressing problem that the Chinese government must solve. （急迫）

9. Following the problem of population increase, the problem of unemployment also arises. （跟着）

10. In this new dormitory, students average 15 square meters of living space. （平均......面积）

七、想一想，说一说：

1．你了解中国人口多的原因吗？

2．你认为人口多好不好？

3．你认为中国政府所采取的控制人口发展的政策好不好？你认为怎样
   做更好？

八、写文章：

在你的国家或地区，哪两个社会问题是当前最急迫需要解决的
问题？仿照本课课文的结构，写一篇短文谈谈这两个问题。

1 · 人口　住房

一、用所給的字組詞：

例：　急---急迫

提---　　　　　　　　　　　　　　　　生---

增---　　　　　　　　　　　　　　　　失---

收---　　　　　　　　　　　　　　　　報---

交---　　　　　　　　　　　　　　　　居---

二、劃線，組成動賓詞組：

增長　　　　　　　　　　　　　　　　影響

提高　　　　　　　　　　　　　　　　政策

提出　　　　　　　　　　　　　　　　水平

解決　　　　　　　　　　　　　　　　收入

帶來　　　　　　　　　　　　　　　　問題

三、選詞填空：

以前......以后　　　　　　　　以前......后來

1· _____他整天玩，不學習，考試成績很不好。今天他下決心，____ 再也不貪玩了。

2· _____他常常開快車，_____出事故了，弄得車毀人傷，他就再也 不敢開快車了。

3· _____我們是好朋友，他去了中國_____，我們就失去了聯系。

4．_____中國的出生率很高，人口增長得很快，_____政府推行了計劃生育的政策，使人口的增長得到了控制。

       平均   平衡

1．在那個地區，人們一年的_____收入是兩千美元。

2．你的飲食結構要_____，既要吃菜，又要吃肉。

3．這個企業今年收支不_____，要虧本了。

4．你這個學期的_____成績是多少分？

       才   就

1．我都等了你二十分鐘了，你_____來呀。

2．我五點_____來了，一直在等你。

3．他讀了三遍那個故事，我_____聽懂。

4．她一個人_____有三套房子。

四、用所給的詞，完成句子：

1．雖然他沒去過中國，_____。（可是）

2．要學好中文，就要_____。（不斷）

3．他讓我上課別遲到，_____。（卻）

4．我們剛剛做了一個聽寫測驗，_____。（跟著）

5．我不喜歡他，_____。（因為）

6．這道題他講了五遍，_____。（還是）

五、造句：

1．可是

2・太

3・跟

4・比如

5・影響

六、用所給詞語將下列句子譯成中文：

1. There are two reports in today's newspaper. The first one concerns the problem of unemployment in the United States; the second one deals with the problem of transportation. （談的是）

2. Chinese is an important language because one out of five people in the world speaks this language. （平均......中）

3. China is confronted with many serious social issues, such as population, housing, corruption, and so on. （比如......等等）

4. The number of students at this university has doubled within three years. （增長）

5. Five years ago, he made only $25,000 a year. Now his annual income has already exceeded $80,000. （超過）

6. The rapid increase in population has created an enormous impact on the living standard of the Chinese people. （帶來）

7. Although the government introduced a special policy to help the poor as early as the late 1970s, poverty still remains a serious social problem in this country. （提出......政策）

8. Presently the shortage of housing is a pressing problem that the Chinese government must solve. （急迫）

9. Following the problem of population increase, the problem of unemployment also arises. （跟著）

10. In this new dormitory, students average 15 square meters of living space. （平均......面積）

七、想一想，説一説：

1．你了解中國人口多的原因嗎？

2．你認為人口多好不好？

3．你認為中國政府所采取的控制人口發展的政策好不好？你認為怎樣做更好？

八、寫文章：

在你的國家或地區，哪兩個社會問題是當前最急迫需要解決的問題？仿照本課課文的結構，寫一篇短文談談這兩個問題。

1·1　人口大爆炸　人口面面观

一、选词填空：

        在......内　　　　　　　　（在）......期间

1·他_____两年_____，就完成了四年的大学课程。

2·_____过去的十年_____，中国的经济有了很大的发展。

3·_____中国留学_____，他交了几个好朋友。

4·_____一个小时_____，你必须写完你的作业。

5·_____休假_____，他读完了两本长篇小说。

二、用所给的词完成句子：

1·他昨天复习功课，一夜没睡觉，_____。（结果）

2·我一次给了我的金鱼很多鱼食，_____。（结果）

3·这篇课文我读了两遍，_____。（仍然）

4·外面在下大雨，他_____。（仍然）

5·大家都知道今天有考试_____。（而）

6·这里夏天的天气很热，_____。（而）

三、造句：

1·如......般（地）

2·分别

3·不过

4·立刻

5·所有的

6·达到

四、看图，用"简直"造句：

（图一）   （图二）

（图三）   （图四）

五、仿照例句，用所给句式或词完成句子：

（一）像......似的，V1+着+V2

例句：他<u>像</u>小兔子<u>似的</u>，<u>跳着</u><u>跑过来</u>。

1. _____，笑着跟我打招呼。

2. _____，一直低着头不说话。

3. 他像听不懂我的话似的，_____。

4. 他像中了乐透奖似的，_____。

5. 他像发疯了似的，_____。

（二）照......下去，就会......。

例句：中国的经济发展得很快，<u>照</u>这样发展<u>下去</u>，不久<u>就会</u>赶
上发达国家。

1. 他要求自己每天记住五十个中文生词，_____。

2. 他开车的速度已达到每小时九十英里了，_____。

3. 我每天只睡三个小时的觉，_____。

（三）......而......，Adj+得+使......受不了

例句：今天的作业很难<u>而</u>又很多，多<u>得</u><u>使</u>我<u>受不了</u>。

1. 那个饭馆的菜很贵，而又难吃，_____。

2. 这个宿舍里很脏，_____。

3. 今年冬天的天气非常干燥，_____。

4. _____，而又很挤，挤得使人们受不了。

六、用所给词语将下列句子译成中文：

1. Don't comment on things that you don't understand. （评价）

2. After the final examinations at the university, Miss Wang and her younger brother each made a phone call to their mother to tell her about their grades. (分别)

3. The members of this government delegation will fly to Beijing on separate airplanes next week. (分别)

4. Even though she didn't like the birthday present her boyfriend gave her, she didn't tell him so because such remarks would make him feel very sad. (使)

5. My older brother made a lot of Chinese friends during the time when he was working in Shanghai. (在 . . . . . . 期间)

6. She promised me that she would finish reading this novel within three days and then return it to me on Friday. (在 . . . . . . 内)

7. He is only a five-year-old kid, but he has memorized nearly one hundred classical Chinese poems. (不过)

8. If the sales of our products keep increasing at this rate, our company will be able to accomplish this year's goal before September. （V＋下去）

9. When my younger sister goes to a department store, she always wants this and that, as if we had a lot of money. （好像……似的）

10. Due to the sudden increase of enrollment this year, the school has to convert many offices into temporary classrooms. （改成）

七、读副课文，回答问题：

1·中国第四次人口调查的结果表明了什么？

2·为什么说在中国实行计划生育是一件了不起的事情？

3·中国的土地面积很大，为什么人口问题还很严重？

4·为什么说九十年代对中国来说，是一个重要的时期？

八、想一想，说一说：

1·在你的国家有人口问题吗？为什么会产生这个问题？

2·你的国家的政府是如何解决人口问题的？

1·1　人口大爆炸　人口面面觀

一、選詞填空：

在.....內　　　　　　　　　（在）.....期間

1·他_____兩年_____，就完成了四年的大學課程。

2·_____過去的十年_____，中國的經濟有了很大的發展。

3·_____中國留學_____，他交了幾個好朋友。

4·_____一個小時_____，你必須寫完你的作業。

5·_____休假_____，他讀完了兩本長篇小說。

二、用所給的詞完成句子：

1·他昨天復習功課，一夜沒睡覺，_____。（結果）

2·我一次給了我的金魚很多魚食，_____。（結果）

3·這篇課文我讀了兩遍，_____。（仍然）

4·外面在下大雨，他_____。（仍然）

5·大家都知道今天有考試_____。（而）

6·這里夏天的天氣很熱，_____。（而）

三、造句：

1·如.....般（地）

2·分別

3·不過

4·立刻

5·所有的

6·達到

四、看圖，用"簡直"造句：

（圖一）　　　　　　　　　（圖二）

（圖三）　　　　　　　　　（圖四）

五、仿照例句，用所給句式或詞完成句子：

　　（一）像......似的，V1+著+V2

例句：他像小兔子似的，跳著 跑過來。

1· _____，笑著跟我打招呼。

2· _____，一直低著頭不說話。

3· 他像聽不懂我的話似的，_____。

4· 他像中了樂透獎似的，_____。

5· 他像發瘋了似的，_____。

（二）照......下去，就會......。

例句：中國的經濟發展得很快，照這樣發展下去，不久就會趕
上發達國家。

1· 他要求自己每天記住五十個中文生詞，_____。

2· 他開車的速度已達到每小時九十英里了，_____。

3· 我每天只睡三個小時的覺，_____。

（三）......而......，Adj+得+使......受不了

例句：今天的作業很難而又很多，多得使我受不了。

1· 那個飯館的菜很貴，而又難吃，_____。

2· 這個宿舍里很髒，_____。

3· 今年冬天的天氣非常干燥，_____。

4· _____，而又很擠，擠得使人們受不了。

六、用所給詞語將下列句子譯成中文：

1. Don't comment on things that you don't understand. （評價）

2. After the final examinations at the university, Miss Wang and her younger brother each made a phone call to their mother to tell her about their grades. (分別)

3. The members of this government delegation will fly to Beijing on separate airplanes next week. (分別)

4. Even though she didn't like the birthday present her boyfriend gave her, she didn't tell him so because such remarks would make him feel very sad. (使)

5. My older brother made a lot of Chinese friends during the time when he was working in Shanghai. (在 . . . . . . 期間)

6. She promised me that she would finish reading this novel within three days and then return it to me on Friday. (在 . . . . . . 內)

7. He is only a five-year-old kid, but he has memorized nearly one hundred classical Chinese poems. (不過)

8. If the sales of our products keep increasing at this rate, our company will be able to accomplish this year's goal before September. （V+下去）

9. When my younger sister goes to a department store, she always wants this and that, as if we had a lot of money. （好像......似的）

10. Due to the sudden increase of enrollment this year, the school has to convert many offices into temporary classrooms. （改成）

七、讀副課文，回答問題：

1・中國第四次人口調查的結果表明了什麼？

2・為什麼說在中國實行計劃生育是一件了不起的事情？

3・中國的土地面積很大，為什麼人口問題還很嚴重？

4・為什麼說九十年代對中國來說，是一個重要的時期？

八、想一想，說一說：

1・在你的國家有人口問題嗎？為什麼會產生這個問題？

2・你的國家的政府是如何解決人口問題的？

1 · 2　住宅

一、划线组词：

（一）
解决	收入
利用	问题
改革	经济
出租	制度
分配	房屋
发展	工作
提高	权力

（解决———问题）

（二）
根本	标准
国际	面积
均等（的）	办法
严重	机会
人均	问题

二、选词填空：

权力　　城市　　住宅　　一套　　存款

解决　　分配　　价格　　买不起　　机会

小王住的_____建了大批_____，小王想买_____

房子，但是他_____，因为房子的_____太高，他在银行里的

_____很少。他想等政府_____给他房子，但是，他手里没有

23

_____，分到房子的_____很少，所以，他不知道怎么才能

_____这个问题。

三、完成句子：

1·这本书是由_____。

2·上大学以来_____。

3·他在大学上课，同时_____。

4·这场大雨造成_____。

5·由于天气太冷，_____。

6·明年我要去中国，一方面_____，另一方面_____，

  同时_____。

7·她不喜欢看外国电影，一个原因是，_____，

  还有一个原因·_____。

四、仿照例句，用所给句式或词造句：

  （一）V + 到

  例句：他听到那个消息后，很高兴。

1·_____。

2·_____。

  （二）V + 不起

  例句：他住不起那么贵的旅馆。

1·_____。

2·_____。

五、造句：

1．甚至

2．利用

3．基本上

4．允许

5．由于

六、读短文，选择正确的答案：

　　中国从一九九八年七月一日起，停止分配国家津贴住房。从九八年下半年开始，国家住房只售卖而不再出租。政府计划把现在的住房租金增至占家庭总收入的百分之十五或市场水平。

　　政府还鼓励居民购买自己的房屋，要使整个国家的住房商品化。

　　回答：从一九九八年下半年开始：

1． A：国家的房屋要分配　　　B：国家的房屋要出租
　　 C：国家停止售卖房子　　　D：国家的房子只售卖

2． A：政府要提高房价　　　　B：政府要降低房价
　　 C：政府要提高房租　　　　D：政府要降低房租

3． A：政府愿意人民买房　　　B：政府不愿意人民 买房
　　 C：政府愿意人民租房　　　D：政府不愿意人民租房

七、就下面这幅画，编一个小对话：

都
市

八、用所给词语将下列句子译成中文：

1. By taking advantage of the power in their hands, some government officials were able to allot government houses to their own children. （利用……权力）

2. After studying Chinese for three years, now he basically has no difficulty communicating with a Chinese person. （基本上）

3. The house price in Shanghai is three to six times more expensive than in Nanjing. （倍）

4. Before the Economic Reform, no one in China could buy a house because the distribution of residential housing was controlled by the government. （ 由 . . . . . . 分配 ）

5. Last year, there appeared a strange phenomenon in this high school: many students began to smoke cigarettes. （ 出现 . . . . . . 现象 ）

6. Our Chinese teacher needs to come up with some good methods to help students to memorize new words. （ 想 . . . . . . 办法 ）

7. Many experts point out that this education system has serious problems, and that the government should find ways to get this system modernized. （ 使 . . . . . . 化 ）

8. In some countries, the rapid increase in population has resulted in the situation of insufficient food and water. （ 造成 . . . . . . 情况 ）

9. There are many reasons why few people want to buy houses. One important reason is that house prices are far beyond the purchasing ability of ordinary people. (多方面)

10. After many complaints had been reported, the mayor finally promised that his government would solve the power shortage problem immediately. (解决)

九、读副课文，回答问题：

1．在中国让市长们最头疼的是什么问题？

2．如果你家是北京的住房困难户，你家平均每人住房面积会是多少？

3．为什么上海外滩一到晚上就会出现"恋爱河岸"的奇观？

4．南京市最近实行的住房政策有哪些新规定？

5．你觉得这个政策可行吗？为什么？

十、想一想，说一说：

1．中国住房紧张，是因为房子建得少吗？

2．中国住房问题存在着什么样的矛盾？

3．你认为中国住房制度应该怎样改革？

4．你的国家有没有住房问题？你们的政府和人民怎样解决这种问题？

1 · 2　住宅

一、劃線組詞：

（一）

解決	收入
利用	問題
改革	經濟
出租	制度
分配	房屋
發展	工作
提高	權力

（二）

根本	標準
國際	面積
均等（的）	辦法
嚴重	機會
人均	問題

二、選詞填空：

權力　　城市　　住宅　　一套　　存款

解決　　分配　　價格　　買不起　　機會

　　小王住的_____建了大批_____，小王想買_____

房子，但是他_____，因為房子的_____太高，他在銀行里的

_____很少。他想等政府_____給他房子，但是，他手里沒有

29

_____，分到房子的_____很少，所以，他不知道怎麼才能
_____這個問題。

三、完成句子：

1·這本書是由_____。

2·上大學以來_____。

3·他在大學上課，同時_____。

4·這場大雨造成_____。

5·由于天氣太冷，_____。

6·明年我要去中國，一方面_____，另一方面_____，
　同時_____。

7·她不喜歡看外國電影，一個原因是，_____，
　還有一個原因，_____。

四、仿照例句，用所給句式或詞造句：

（一）V + 到

例句：他<u>聽到</u>那個消息後，很高興。

1·_____。

2·_____。

（二）V + 不起

例句：他<u>住不起</u>那麼貴的旅館。

1·_____。

2·_____。

五、造句：

1‧甚至

2‧利用

3‧基本上

4‧允許

5‧由于

六、讀短文，選擇正確的答案：

中國從一九九八年七月一日起，停止分配國家津貼住房。從九八年下半年開始，國家住房只售賣而不再出租。政府計劃把現在的住房租金增至佔家庭總收入的百分之十五或市場水平。

政府還鼓勵居民購買自己的房屋，要使整個國家的住房商品化。

回答：從一九九八年下半年開始：

1‧ A：國家的房屋要分配　　　B：國家的房屋要出租
　　C：國家停止售賣房子　　　D：國家的房子只售賣

2‧ A：政府要提高房價　　　　B：政府要降低房價
　　C：政府要提高房租　　　　D：政府要降低房租

3‧ A：政府願意人民買房　　　B：政府不願意人民 買房
　　C：政府願意人民租房　　　D：政府不願意人民租房

七、就下面這幅畫，編一個小對話：

都
市

八、用所給詞語將下列句子譯成中文：

1. By taking advantage of the power in their hands, some government officials were able to allot government houses to their own children. （利用......權力）

2. After studying Chinese for three years, now he basically has no difficulty communicating with a Chinese person. （基本上）

3. The house price in Shanghai is three to six times more expensive than in Nanjing. （倍）

4. Before the Economic Reform, no one in China could buy a house because the distribution of residential housing was controlled by the government. （由......分配 ）

5. Last year, there appeared a strange phenomenon in this high school: many students began to smoke cigarettes. （出現......現象 ）

6. Our Chinese teacher needs to come up with some good methods to help students to memorize new words. （想......辦法 ）

7. Many experts point out that this education system has serious problems, and that the government should find ways to get this system modernized. （使......化 ）

8. In some countries, the rapid increase in population has resulted in the situation of insufficient food and water. （造成......情況 ）

9. There are many reasons why few people want to buy houses. One important reason is that house prices are far beyond the purchasing ability of ordinary people. (多方面)

10. After many complaints had been reported, the mayor finally promised that his government would solve the power shortage problem immediately. （解決）

九、讀副課文，回答問題：

1・在中國讓市長們最頭疼的是什麼問題？

2・如果你家是北京的住房困難戶，你家平均每人住房面積會是多少？

3・為什麼上海外灘一到晚上就會出現 " 戀愛河岸 " 的奇觀？

4・南京市最近實行的住房政策有哪些新規定？

5・你覺得這個政策可行嗎？為什麼？

十、想一想，說一說：

1・中國住房緊張，是因為房子建得少嗎？

2・中國住房問題存在著什麼樣的矛盾？

3・你認為中國住房制度應該怎樣改革？

4・你的國家有沒有住房問題？你們的政府和人民怎樣解決這種問題？

2・ 教育   就业

一、写出反义词：

落后---　　　　　　　　　　　　收入---

发展---　　　　　　　　　　　　出现---

下降---　　　　　　　　　　　　迅速---

新---　　　　　　　　　　　　　差---

二、选词填空：

重视　　　　　迅速　　　　　条件　　　　　特别

出现　　　　　必须　　　　　达到　　　　　反映

1・近几年来，中国的高科技_____发展。

2・一个国家要发展，必须_____教育问题。

3・雨后，天边_____了一道彩虹。

4・那里的_____不好，她不愿意去那里工作。

5・我喜欢旅游，_____是喜欢到有山的地方去。

6・明天有考试，你_____来上课。

7・这篇报道很不错，真实地_____了中国目前的人口问题。

8・你的汉语学得很好，已经_____了高级汉语的水平。

三、完成句子：

1・在过去的_____里，人类文明有了前所未有的进步。

2・在今后的_____里，中国的经济将会有更大的发展。

3・在_____期间，美国的失业率下降到了近五十年来的最低点。

4・在_____期间，他参观了很多那儿的名胜古迹。

5・所有的美国公民都必须_____。

6・在这个州，所有拥有枪枝的人都必须_____。

四、造句：

1・有的......有的......

2・拿......来说

3・越......越......

4・于是

5・实行

五、用所给词语将下列句子译成中文：

1. After the newspaper reported that he had given a government house to his son, the mayor's reputation was greatly damaged. （受.....损害）

2. In recent years, the local government of my hometown has increased funds for education. Take last year for example: three new elementary schools were set up. （拿......来说）

3. You will never learn Chinese well if you don't pay attention to basic skills in writing characters and pronunciation. （重视）

4. After more than twenty years of rural economic reform, the number of poor people has dropped to about six percent of the entire rural population. （下降......左右）

5. The economic situation in this city was so bad that by the end of last year, the number of unemployed workers had reached 150,000. （达到）

6. The policy of a nine-year compulsory education was implemented in China during the 1980s. （实行）

7. It is a pity that many children quit school because their parents think going to school is useless. （认为）

8. Since the end of the Cultural Revolution, education in China has developed rapidly. Various kinds of schools have appeared. （发展）

9. This American university has many foreign students. Some are from European countries, some are from African countries, while the majority of them are from Asian countries. （有的......有的......）

10. The report introduces the current situation of China's economic reform in different aspects. （从......方面）

六、 想一想，说一说：

1．你认为中国政府应该怎样解决近几年出现的教育方面的新问题。

2．在你的国家，政府是如何对待教育问题的？

七、写文章：

一个国家的教育跟政治、经济有什么关系？如果一个国家的教育落后，主要的原因会是什么？一个国家的经济发展了，教育也一定会发展吗？写一篇短文谈谈这些问题，并根据你的经历，举例说明。

2・教育　就業

一、寫出反義詞：

落后---　　　　　　　　　　收入---

發展---　　　　　　　　　　出現---

下降 ---　　　　　　　　　　迅速---

新---　　　　　　　　　　　差 ---

二、選詞填空：

重視　　　　　迅速　　　　　條件　　　　　特別

出現　　　　　必須　　　　　達到　　　　　反映

1・近幾年來，中國的高科技_____發展。

2・一個國家要發展，必須_____教育問題。

3・雨后，天邊_____了一道彩虹。

4・那里的_____不好，她不願意去那里工作。

5・我喜歡旅遊，_____是喜歡到有山的地方去。

6・明天有考試，你_____來上課。

7・這篇報道很不錯，真實地_____了中國目前的人口問題。

8・你的漢語學得很好，已經_____了高級漢語的水平。

三、完成句子：

1・在過去的_____里，人類文明有了前所未有的進步。

2・在今后的_____里，中國的經濟將會有更大的發展。

3．在_____期間，美國的失業率下降到了近五十年來的最低點。

4．在_____期間，他參觀了很多那兒的名勝古跡。

5．所有的美國公民都必須_____。

6．在這個州，所有擁有槍枝的人都必須_____。

四、造句：

1．有的......有的......

2．拿......來説

3．越......越......

4．于是

5．實行

五、用所給詞語將下列句子譯成中文：

1. After the newspaper reported that he had given a government house to his son, the mayor's reputation was greatly damaged. （受......損害）

2. In recent years, the local government of my hometown has increased funds for education. Take last year for example: three new elementary schools were set up. （拿......來説）

3. You will never learn Chinese well if you don't pay attention to basic skills in writing characters and pronunciation. （重視）

4. After more than twenty years of rural economic reform, the number of poor people has dropped to about six percent of the entire rural population. （下降......左右）

5. The economic situation in this city was so bad that by the end of last year, the number of unemployed workers had reached 150,000. （達到）

6. The policy of a nine-year compulsory education was implemented in China during the 1980s. （實行）

7. It is a pity that many children quit school because their parents think going to school is useless. （認為）

8. Since the end of the Cultural Revolution, education in China has developed rapidly. Various kinds of schools have appeared. （發展）

9. This American university has many foreign students. Some are from European countries, some are from African countries, while the majority of them are from Asian countries. （有的......有的......）

10. The report introduces the current situation of China's economic reform in different aspects. （從......方面）

六、 想一想，説一説：

1．你認為中國政府應該怎樣解決近几年出現的教育方面的新問題。

2．在你的國家，政府是如何對待教育問題的？

七、寫文章：

一個國家的教育跟政治、經濟有什麼關系？如果一個國家的教育落后，主要的原因會是什麼？一個國家的經濟發展了，教育也一定會發展嗎？寫一篇短文談談這些問題，並根據你的經歷，舉例説明。

2·1　我是职业高中生

一、给下列划线的词注上拼音：

1·　不劳动不<u>得</u>食。

　　她长<u>得</u>真漂亮。

2·　你<u>了</u>解中国历史吗？

　　我看完<u>了</u>那本书。

3·　我们今天下午三点开<u>会</u>。

　　他是学财<u>会</u>的学生。

二、仿照例句，用所给句式或词造句：

　　（一）Adj＋是＋Adj，可是......

　　例句：他的工作累<u>是</u>累，<u>可是</u>很有意思。

1·＿＿＿＿＿＿＿＿＿＿＿＿＿＿＿＿＿＿＿＿＿＿＿＿＿。

2·＿＿＿＿＿＿＿＿＿＿＿＿＿＿＿＿＿＿＿＿＿＿＿＿＿。

　　（二）离......（只、还、就）有......

　　例句：这里<u>离</u>飞机场还<u>有</u>二十英里。

1·＿＿＿＿＿＿＿＿＿＿＿＿＿＿＿＿＿＿＿＿＿＿＿＿＿。

2·＿＿＿＿＿＿＿＿＿＿＿＿＿＿＿＿＿＿＿＿＿＿＿＿＿。

三、仿照例句，用划线的词造句：

1·<u>即使</u>考不上，心里<u>也</u>不会太难过。

2·利用暑假为个体户结账，检查仓库，<u>既</u>实际，<u>又</u>得钱。

3·<u>无论</u>什么人，听说我学会计<u>都</u>说："好！"

4·我每天<u>除了</u>上课，<u>就是</u>做功课。

四、完成句子：

1·他自己做错了事，反而＿＿＿＿＿＿＿＿＿＿＿＿＿＿＿＿＿＿＿＿＿。

2·＿＿＿＿＿＿＿＿＿＿＿＿＿＿＿＿＿＿＿＿＿，简直受不了啦。

3·＿＿＿＿＿＿＿＿＿＿＿＿＿＿＿＿＿＿＿，真是一举两得。

4·＿＿＿＿＿＿＿＿＿＿＿＿＿＿＿＿＿＿，我很惋惜。

5·＿＿＿＿＿＿＿＿＿＿＿＿＿＿＿＿＿，喘不过气来。

6·下雨了，我只好＿＿＿＿＿＿＿＿＿＿＿＿＿＿＿＿＿＿＿。

7·＿＿＿＿＿＿＿＿＿＿＿＿＿＿＿＿＿＿，他真是太幸运了。

五、仿照例句，用"跟……相比"造句：

例：我的家乡……纽约

→ 我的家乡跟纽约相比，人很少，也很安静。

1·学中文……学英文

2·中国……美国

3·美国的南方……美国的北方

4·熊猫……熊

5·做生意……当老师

六、看图，用"简直受不了啦"造句子：

（图一）　　　　　　　　（图二）

（图三）　　　　　　　　（图四）

七、用所给词语将下列句子译成中文：

1. No one can deny that he is the best basketball player in our school, even though he is not on the school team. （否认）

2. After eating and relaxing in the fast food restaurant, they continued driving on the highway to Canada. （继续）

3. Students complain that the university's dining room has nothing but rice and noodles every day. （除了......就是......）

4. The girl began to take piano lessons two years later than her older brother, but she plays piano much better than he. （反而）

5. According to today's newspaper, this company will go ahead with its plan to build two hundred houses this year, even if it does not get the government's support. （即使......也......）

6. He feels that he knows very little about Chinese culture even though he has spent a summer in China. （了解）

7. No matter where I go, I can not find a place as beautiful as my hometown. （无论）

8. He plans to go to Taiwan to teach English while studying Chinese there. He thinks this terrific plan is like killing two birds with one stone. （一举两得）

9. Taking the opportunity of attending a conference in New York, he visited several old friends and went to see a play in a famous theater. （利用）

10. If you go to Beijing, you should visit the Great Wall and the Forbidden City. Otherwise, you would regret it later on. （遗憾）

八、读副课文，回答问题：

1·中华社会大学与其他的大学有什么不同？

2·这所大学的学生与一般大学的学生有什么不同？

3·这所大学的毕业生到社会上受欢迎吗？为什么？

九、想一想，说一说：

1·你有过什么"遗憾"的事情吗？

2·你有什么"烦恼"吗？

2‧1 我是職業高中生

一、給下列劃線的詞注上拼音：

1‧ 不勞動不<u>得</u>食。

她長<u>得</u>真漂亮。

2‧ 你<u>了</u>解中國歷史嗎？

我看完<u>了</u>那本書。

3‧ 我們今天下午三點開<u>會</u>。

他是學財<u>會</u>的學生。

二、仿照例句，用所給句式或詞造句：

（一）Adj＋是＋Adj，可是......

例句：他的工作累是累，<u>可是</u>很有意思。

1‧＿＿＿＿＿＿＿＿＿＿＿＿＿＿＿＿＿＿＿＿＿＿＿＿＿＿＿＿＿＿＿＿＿。

2‧＿＿＿＿＿＿＿＿＿＿＿＿＿＿＿＿＿＿＿＿＿＿＿＿＿＿＿＿＿＿＿＿＿。

（二）離......（只、還、就）有......

例句：這里<u>離</u>飛機場還<u>有</u>二十英里。

1‧＿＿＿＿＿＿＿＿＿＿＿＿＿＿＿＿＿＿＿＿＿＿＿＿＿＿＿＿＿＿＿＿＿。

2‧＿＿＿＿＿＿＿＿＿＿＿＿＿＿＿＿＿＿＿＿＿＿＿＿＿＿＿＿＿＿＿＿＿。

三、仿照例句，用劃線的詞造句：

1‧<u>即使</u>考不上，心里<u>也</u>不會太難過。

49

2・利用暑假為個體戶結賬，檢查倉庫，既實際，又得錢。

3・無論什麼人，聽說我學會計都說："好！"

4・我每天除了上課，就是做功課。

四、完成句子：

1・他自己做錯了事，反而_____。

2・_____，簡直受不了啦。

3・_____，真是一舉兩得。

4・_____，我很惋惜。

5・_____，喘不過氣來。

6・下雨了，我只好_____。

7・_____，他真是太幸運了。

五、仿照例句，用"跟......相比"造句：

例：我的家鄉......紐約

→我的家鄉跟紐約相比，人很少，也很安靜。

1・學中文......學英文

2・中國......美國

3・美國的南方......美國的北方

4・熊貓......熊

5・做生意......當老師

六、看圖，用 " 簡直受不了啦 " 造句子：

（圖一）　　　　　　　　　　（圖二）

（圖三）　　　　　　　　　　（圖四）

七、用所給詞語將下列句子譯成中文：

1. No one can deny that he is the best basketball player in our school, even
    though he is not on the school team. （否認）

2. After eating and relaxing in the fast food restaurant, they continued driving on the highway to Canada. （繼續）

3. Students complain that the university's dining room has nothing but rice and noodles every day. （除了......就是......）

4. The girl began to take piano lessons two years later than her older brother, but she plays piano much better than he. （反而）

5. According to today's newspaper, this company will go ahead with its plan to build two hundred houses this year, even if it does not get the government's support. （即使......也......）

6. He feels that he knows very little about Chinese culture even though he has spent a summer in China. （了解）

7. No matter where I go, I can not find a place as beautiful as my hometown. （無論）

8. He plans to go to Taiwan to teach English while studying Chinese there. He thinks this terrific plan is like killing two birds with one stone. （一舉兩得）

9. Taking the opportunity of attending a conference in New York, he visited several old friends and went to see a play in a famous theater. （利用）

10. If you go to Beijing, you should visit the Great Wall and the Forbidden City. Otherwise, you would regret it later on. （遺憾）

八、讀副課文，回答問題：

1·中華社會大學與其他的大學有什麼不同？

2·這所大學的學生與一般大學的學生有什麼不同？

3·這所大學的畢業生到社會上受歡迎嗎？為什麼？

九、想一想，說一說：

1·你有過什麼"遺憾"的事情嗎？

2·你有什麼"煩惱"嗎？

2·2 从"退学风"到"考研热"

一、用中文解释下列各词：

前所未有   重点大学   本科生

中外合资   自费留学   考研热

二、选词填空：

需求 毕业 工资 要求 对……来说

理想 增加 研究生 合适 中外合资

小李是一名本科毕业生，_____后，他一直没有找到工作。他想去_____的企业工作，在那里_____会很高，工作条件也很_____。虽然那些企业对人才的_____一年比一年_____，可是他们对人才的学历_____也比较高，这_____小李_____是一个困难。于是小李决定，要是没有_____的工作，那他就去读_____。

三、仿照例句，用所给句式或词完成句子：

（一）仅……就……

例句：仅用了两年时间，他就完成了四年的大学课程。

1·我们的中文课学得很快，_____。

2·他仅学了一年中文，_____。

3·那个饭馆的菜都很贵，_____。

4．现在交通工具很发达，_____。

（二）对......来说，当然......

例句：对学生来说，学习成绩当然很重要。

1．对一个国家的总统来说，_____。

2．对记者来说，_____。

3．对老师来说，_____。

4．能不能有一个安定富裕的生活，对老百姓来说_____

_____。

（三）比......差得多

例句：在中国，很多人不愿意去农村工作，因为那里的生活条
件比大城市的差得多。

1．在这个公司里，不同学历的人待遇不一样，_____。

2．他很长时间没来上课，_____。

3．在中国，以前一些有权力的人，专为自己谋私利，在住房方面___

_____。

4．自从他生了那场大病以后，_____。

（四）......，甚至......

例句：他不吃那种菜，甚至闻到那种菜的味儿都受不了。

1．他工作非常忙，_____。

2．在中外合资企业工作比在国营企业工作，工资高得多，_____。

3．他非常想到中国去，_____。

4．他很穷，_____。

四、造句：

1. 前所未有

2. 特别

3. 增加

4. 自动

5. 资格

6. 规定

五、完成句子和对话：

1. _____，以学习为主。

2. 为了找到一个理想的工作，_____。

3. _____，他的妈妈感到很光荣。

4. _____，一天比一天冷。

5. 他告诉我上课别迟到，他居然_____。

6. 天气预报说，今天是晴天，居然_____。

7. _____，他居然不知道。

8. A：你想退学，告诉你妈妈了吗？

   B：_____。（当然）

9. A：这么多的饭，你吃得完吗？

   B：_____。（当然）

10. 出国留学好是好，_____。

六、看图，用"一......就"回答问题：

1·下班后，他马上去做什么？

2·他做买卖做得怎么样？

3·他们俩第一次见面，互相觉得怎么样？

4 . 他听到那个坏消息后，怎么了？

5 . 他闻到花粉时，会怎么样？

6 . 这条狗见到人的时候，它做什么？

七、用所给词语将下列句子译成中文：

1. At this national math competition, Miss Wang won the first place with the best score ever. （前所未有）

2. Twenty-two employees left this advertising company for better-paid jobs within only one week. （仅......就有）

3. According to the university's regulations, M.A. students have to complete at least thirty credit hours in their home departments to get the master's degree. （规定）

4. He just turned 18 years old last week, and is qualified to participate and vote in this election. （有资格）

5. It is up to the doctor to make the decision whether this child should be released from the hospital today. （由......决定）

6. In contrast to the rapid increase of his wealth, his health is deteriorating day by day. （一天比一天）

7. The 6-year old boy was so brave that he even dared to touch the huge snake on the show. （居然）

8. Members of this drama club mainly consist of students of our university, but the club has also attracted some teachers who enjoy dramatic

performance.（以......为主）

9. We haven't corresponded with each other for over five years now. He doesn't even know that I already got married and started a family. （甚至）

10. Based on the introduction by the tourist guide, this Buddhist temple has existed for over 1,000 years and is a symbol of this small town's long history.（据......介绍）

八、读副课文，回答问题：

1·中国的大学近几年来有哪些方面的变化？

2·为什么国家要在收费方面改变以前的规定？

3·学生毕业以后怎样找工作？

4·在大学中出现了什么前所未有的现象？

5·中美的大学教育有什么异同？

九、想一想，说一说：

1·"退学风"和"考研热"在不同的时期出现，与中国的经济改革有

没有关系？有什么关系？

2·你是根据什么来选择自己的专业的？

3·谈谈"理想的职业"。

2·2　從"退學風"到"考研熱"

一、用中文解釋下列各詞：

前所未有　　　　　重點大學　　　　　本科生

中外合資　　　　　自費留學　　　　　考研熱

二、選詞填空：

需求　　　畢業　　　工資　　　要求　　　對……來說

理想　　　增加　　　研究生　　　合適　　　中外合資

小李是一名本科畢業生，_____后，他一直沒有找到工作。他想去_____的企業工作，在那里_____會很高，工作條件也很_____。雖然那些企業對人才的_____一年比一年_____，可是他們對人才的學歷_____也比較高，這_____小李_____是一個困難。于是小李決定，要是沒有_____的工作，那他就去讀_____。

三、仿照例句，用所給句式或詞完成句子：

（一）僅……就……

例句：僅用了兩年時間，他就完成了四年的大學課程。

1·我們的中文課學得很快，_____。

2·他僅學了一年中文，_____。

3·那個飯館的菜都很貴，_____。

4．現在交通工具很發達，＿＿＿＿＿＿＿＿＿＿＿＿＿＿＿＿＿＿＿＿＿＿。

（二）對......來説，當然......

例句：對學生來説，學習成績當然很重要。

1．對一個國家的總統來説，＿＿＿＿＿＿＿＿＿＿＿＿＿＿＿＿＿＿＿。

2．對記者來説，＿＿＿＿＿＿＿＿＿＿＿＿＿＿＿＿＿＿＿＿＿＿＿＿。

3．對老師來説，＿＿＿＿＿＿＿＿＿＿＿＿＿＿＿＿＿＿＿＿＿＿＿＿。

4．能不能有一個安定富裕的生活，對老百姓來説＿＿＿＿＿＿＿＿＿＿

＿＿＿＿＿＿＿＿＿＿＿＿＿。

（三）比......差得多

例句：在中國，很多人不願意去農村工作，因為那里的生活條

件比大城市的差得多。

1．在這個公司里，不同學歷的人待遇不一樣，＿＿＿＿＿＿＿＿＿。

2．他很長時間沒來上課，＿＿＿＿＿＿＿＿＿＿＿＿＿＿＿＿＿＿＿。

3．在中國，以前一些有權力的人，專為自己謀私利，在住房方面＿＿

＿＿＿＿＿＿＿＿＿＿＿＿＿。

4．自從他生了那場大病以后，＿＿＿＿＿＿＿＿＿＿＿＿＿＿＿＿＿。

（四）......，甚至......

例句：他不吃那種菜，甚至聞到那種菜的味兒都受不了。

1．他工作非常忙，＿＿＿＿＿＿＿＿＿＿＿＿＿＿＿＿＿＿＿＿＿＿。

2．在中外合資企業工作比在國營企業工作，工資高得多，＿＿＿＿。

3．他非常想到中國去，＿＿＿＿＿＿＿＿＿＿＿＿＿＿＿＿＿＿＿＿。

4．他很窮，＿＿＿＿＿＿＿＿＿＿＿＿＿＿＿＿＿＿＿＿＿＿＿＿＿。

四、造句：

1· 前所未有

2· 特別

3· 增加

4· 自動

5· 資格

6· 規定

五、完成句子和對話：

1·＿＿＿＿＿＿＿＿＿＿＿＿＿＿＿＿＿＿＿，以學習為主。

2· 為了找到一個理想的工作，＿＿＿＿＿＿＿＿＿＿＿＿＿＿。

3·＿＿＿＿＿＿＿＿＿＿＿＿＿＿＿，他的媽媽感到很光榮。

4·＿＿＿＿＿＿＿＿＿＿＿＿＿＿，一天比一天冷。

5· 他告訴我上課別遲到，他居然＿＿＿＿＿＿＿＿＿＿＿。

6· 天氣預報說，今天是晴天，居然＿＿＿＿＿＿＿＿＿＿＿。

7·＿＿＿＿＿＿＿＿＿＿＿＿＿＿，他居然不知道。

8· A：你想退學，告訴你媽媽了嗎？

   B：＿＿＿＿＿＿＿＿＿＿＿＿＿＿＿。（當然）

9· A：這麼多的飯，你吃得完嗎？

   B：＿＿＿＿＿＿＿＿＿＿＿＿＿＿。（當然）

10· 出國留學好是好，＿＿＿＿＿＿＿＿＿＿＿＿＿＿。

六、看圖，用" 一⋯⋯就 "回答問題：

1．下班後，他馬上去做什麼？

2．他做買賣做得怎麼樣？

3．他們倆第一次見面，互相覺得怎麼樣？

4．他聽到那個壞消息後，怎麼了？

5．他聞到花粉時，會怎麼樣？

6．這條狗見到人的時候，它做什麼？

七、用所給詞語將下列句子譯成中文：

1. At this national math competition, Miss Wang won the first place with the best score ever. （前所未有）

2. Twenty-two employees left this advertising company for better-paid jobs within only one week. （僅......就有）

3. According to the university's regulations, M.A. students have to complete at least thirty credit hours in their home departments to get the master's degree. （規定）

4. He just turned 18 years old last week, and is qualified to participate and vote in this election. （有資格）

5. It is up to the doctor to make the decision whether this child should be released from the hospital today. （由......決定）

6. In contrast to the rapid increase of his wealth, his health is deteriorating day by day. （一天比一天）

7. The 6-year old boy was so brave that he even dared to touch the huge snake on the show. （居然）

8. Members of this drama club mainly consist of students of our university, but the club has also attracted some teachers who enjoy dramatic

performance. （以......為主）

9. We haven't corresponded with each other for over five years now. He doesn't even know that I already got married and started a family. （甚至）

10. Based on the introduction by the tourist guide, this Buddhist temple has existed for over 1,000 years and is a symbol of this small town's long history. （據......介紹）

八、讀副課文，回答問題：

1·中國的大學近幾年來有哪些方面的變化？

2·為什麼國家要在收費方面改變以前的規定？

3·學生畢業以后怎樣找工作？

4·在大學中出現了什麼前所未有的現象？

5·中美的大學教育有什麼異同？

九、想一想，說一說：

1· "退學風" 和 "考研熱" 在不同的時期出現，與中國的經濟改革有

沒有關系？有什麼關系？

2·你是根據什麼來選擇自己的專業的？

3·談談 "理想的職業" 。

2·3 "读书无用"论的新冲击

一、划线，组成词组：

一对 ——————————— 宾馆

一位 ——————————— 夫妇

一间 楼房

一栋 屋子

一家 工程师

二、仿照例子，组成动宾词组：

例：<u>赚</u>钱

_____钱 _____钱 _____钱

_____钱 _____钱 _____钱

三、选词填空：

变化 人才 待遇 骄傲

水平 难过 考虑 决定

1·我来这里工作，不是为了好的_____，只是为了好的环境。

2·妈妈为儿子取得的好成绩感到_____。

3·她的试验又没有成功，她感到_____。

4·这几年，中国在经济方面发生了很大_____，人民

的生活_____有了很大提高。

5·这个学校为社会培养了很多_____。

6·这个问题，你要认真_____以后，才能_____。

四、仿照例句，用所给的句式或词完成句子：

（一）除了......没有......

例句：她每天除了工作，没有时间做别的事情。

1·这个商店除了彩电、电冰箱，_____。

2·除了周末，他_____。

3·在中国，除了改革开放，_____。

4·除了计划生育，_____。

（二）......之后，却又......

例句：以前，他很喜欢自己的专业，可是工作之后，却又对自己

选择的专业后悔了。

1·他觉得这本书很有意思，_____。

2·他以为自己的汉语说得不错了，_____。

3·我花很多钱买了那个艺术品，_____。

4·上大学以前，他一直想赶快离开父母，_____。

（三）别说......就是......也......

例句：他刚学了两个月汉语，别说当翻译，就是和别人简单地对

话，也还有问题。

1·他的工资很少，_____。

2·他没有文化，_____。

3·这个道理很简单，_____。

4·我每天的工作很忙，_____。

五、用指定的词完成句子：

1 · 我没有钱，_____。（V+不起）

2 · 我不能帮你做这件事，因为责任太大了，_____。（V+不起）

3 · _____，他很难过。（失利）

4 · 这场比赛很重要，_____。（失利）

5 · 他工作很多年了，挣的钱却很少，还_____。（不如）

6 · 他十岁了，他的弟弟才八岁，可是_____。（不如）

7 · 他八十岁了，_____。（一直）

8 · 我们在网络上通信交往已经两年了，可是_____。（一直）

9 · _____，我不吸烟了。（自从......之后）

10 · _____他们一直没见过面。（自从......之后）

六、用所给词语将下列句子译成中文：

1. After traveling two months on foot, we almost had nothing left except a map of the desert and a flashlight. （除了......没有......）

2. All the students feel heartbroken, because the women's basketball team of the university lost in yesterday's game. （失利）

3. The university takes great pride in its academic achievements over the past decade. （骄傲）

4. This couple came back from China yesterday. They said that tremendous changes have taken place in China since they first visited that country ten years ago. （发生......变化）

5. Everyone here knows that the old man is the richest person in town. Strangely, however, his house does not even look as good as the houses of some poor people. （还不如）

6. Mr. and Mrs. Wang are considered a model couple by their relatives and friends because they have never quarreled ever since they were married twenty years ago. （自从......以后）

7. This young couple had been out of work for six months. They couldn't even rent an apartment, not to mention buying a new car.
（别说......就是......也......）

8. After careful consideration, she decided to go to graduate school after completing her undergraduate studies, rather than working as a secretary in a law firm. （考虑）

9. The main character is a poor boy in a certain city in China. The story is about how he avenges the death of his father after he grows up. （某）

10. He has worked for the bank since it was founded forty years ago, and has made great contributions to its development. （为．．．．．作出贡献）

七、读副课文，回答问题：

1．十年前的中国是什么情况？改革后，中国出现了什么现象？

2．卖菜的那个学生，以前学习怎么样？现在他的工作怎么样？

3．老师遇到那个学生后，为什么心里不平静？

4．你对中国的这个现象有什么看法？

八、想一想，说一说：

1．课文中为什么说"读书无用"论是新冲击？你知道中国历史上还有什么时候有过这种情况？

2．为什么中国会出现"读书无用"论？你认为如何才能消除这种现象？

3．你认为现在的社会中一个人的文化水平一定会和经济收入成正比吗？

4．你为自己、或你的亲人、你的民族、你的国家的什么事情而骄傲？

5．你有过难过的时候吗？你为什么感到难过？

2·3　"讀書無用"論的新沖擊

一、劃線，組成詞組：

一對　　　　　　　　　　　賓館

一位　　　　　　　　　　　夫婦

一間　　　　　　　　　　　樓房

一棟　　　　　　　　　　　屋子

一家　　　　　　　　　　　工程師

二、仿照例子，組成動賓詞組：

例：賺錢

_____錢　　　　　_____錢　　　　　_____錢

_____錢　　　　　_____錢　　　　　_____錢

三、選詞填空：

變化　　　　人才　　　　待遇　　　　驕傲

水平　　　　難過　　　　考慮　　　　決定

1·我來這里工作，不是為了好的_____，只是為了好的環境。

2·媽媽為兒子取得的好成績感到_____。

3·她的試驗又沒有成功，她感到_____。

4·這几年，中國在經濟方面發生了很大_____，人民

的生活_____有了很大提高。

5·這個學校為社會培養了很多_____。

6‧這個問題，你要認真＿＿＿＿＿＿＿以后，才能＿＿＿＿＿＿＿。

四、仿照例句，用所給的句式或詞完成句子：

（一）除了......沒有......

例句：她每天除了工作，沒有時間做別的事情。

1‧這個商店除了彩電、電冰箱，＿＿＿＿＿＿＿＿＿＿＿＿＿＿＿。

2‧除了周末，他＿＿＿＿＿＿＿＿＿＿＿＿＿＿＿＿＿＿＿＿＿。

3‧在中國，除了改革開放，＿＿＿＿＿＿＿＿＿＿＿＿＿＿＿＿＿。

4‧除了計劃生育，＿＿＿＿＿＿＿＿＿＿＿＿＿＿＿＿＿＿＿＿＿。

（二）......之后，卻又......

例句：以前，他很喜歡自己的專業，可是工作之后，卻又對自己
選擇的專業后悔了。

1‧他覺得這本書很有意思，＿＿＿＿＿＿＿＿＿＿＿＿＿＿＿＿＿。

2‧他以為自己的漢語說得不錯了，＿＿＿＿＿＿＿＿＿＿＿＿＿＿。

3‧我花很多錢買了那個藝術品，＿＿＿＿＿＿＿＿＿＿＿＿＿＿＿。

4‧上大學以前，他一直想趕快離開父母，＿＿＿＿＿＿＿＿＿＿＿。

（三）別說......就是......也......

例句：他剛學了兩個月漢語，別說當翻譯，就是和別人簡單地對
話，也還有問題。

1‧他的工資很少，＿＿＿＿＿＿＿＿＿＿＿＿＿＿＿＿＿＿＿＿＿。

2‧他沒有文化，＿＿＿＿＿＿＿＿＿＿＿＿＿＿＿＿＿＿＿＿＿＿。

3‧這個道理很簡單，＿＿＿＿＿＿＿＿＿＿＿＿＿＿＿＿＿＿＿＿。

4‧我每天的工作很忙，＿＿＿＿＿＿＿＿＿＿＿＿＿＿＿＿＿＿＿。

五、用指定的詞完成句子：

1‧我沒有錢，＿＿＿＿＿＿＿＿＿＿＿＿＿＿＿＿＿＿＿＿＿。（V+不起）

2‧我不能幫你做這件事，因為責任太大了，＿＿＿＿＿＿＿。（V+不起）

3‧＿＿＿＿＿＿＿＿＿＿＿＿＿＿＿＿＿＿＿＿＿＿＿，他很難過。（失利）

4‧這場比賽很重要，＿＿＿＿＿＿＿＿＿＿＿＿＿＿＿＿＿。（失利）

5‧他工作很多年了，掙的錢卻很少，還＿＿＿＿＿＿＿＿＿。（不如）

6‧他十歲了，他的弟弟才八歲，可是＿＿＿＿＿＿＿＿＿。（不如）

7‧他八十歲了，＿＿＿＿＿＿＿＿＿＿＿＿＿＿＿＿＿＿＿。（一直）

8‧我們在網絡上通信交往已經兩年了，可是＿＿＿＿＿＿＿。（一直）

9‧＿＿＿＿＿＿＿＿＿＿＿＿＿＿＿＿＿，我不吸煙了。（自從......之后）

10‧＿＿＿＿＿＿＿＿＿＿＿＿＿＿＿他們一直沒見過面。（自從......之后）

六、用所給詞語將下列句子譯成中文：

1. After traveling two months on foot, we almost had nothing left except a map of the desert and a flashlight. （除了......沒有......）

2. All the students feel heartbroken, because the women's basketball team of the university lost in yesterday's game. （失利）

3. The university takes great pride in its academic achievements over the past decade. （驕傲）

4. This couple came back from China yesterday. They said that tremendous changes have taken place in China since they first visited that country ten years ago. （發生......變化）

5. Everyone here knows that the old man is the richest person in town. Strangely, however, his house does not even look as good as the houses of some poor people. （還不如）

6. Mr. and Mrs. Wang are considered a model couple by their relatives and friends because they have never quarreled ever since they were married twenty years ago. （自從......以后）

7. This young couple had been out of work for six months. They couldn't even rent an apartment, not to mention buying a new car.
   （別說......就是......也......）

8. After careful consideration, she decided to go to graduate school after completing her undergraduate studies, rather than working as a secretary in a law firm. （考慮）

9. The main character is a poor boy in a certain city in China. The story is about how he avenges the death of his father after he grows up. （某）

10. He has worked for the bank since it was founded forty years ago, and has made great contributions to its development. （為......作出貢獻）

七、讀副課文，回答問題：

1·十年前的中國是什麼情況？改革後，中國出現了什麼現象？

2·賣菜的那個學生，以前學習怎麼樣？現在他的工作怎麼樣？

3·老師遇到那個學生後，為什麼心里不平靜？

4·你對中國的這個現象有什麼看法？

八、想一想，説一説：

1·課文中為什麼説"讀書無用"論是新沖擊？你知道中國歷史上還有什麼時候有過這種情況？

2·為什麼中國會出現"讀書無用"論？你認為如何才能消除這種現象？

3·你認為現在的社會中一個人的文化水平一定會和經濟收入成正比嗎？

4·你為自己、或你的親人、你的民族、你的國家的什麼事情而驕傲？

5·你有過難過的時候嗎？你為什麼感到難過？

3 · 恋爱　婚姻

一、划线组词：

（1）　　限制　　　　　　　　幸福

　　　　改变　　　　　　　　思想

　　　　压抑　　　　　　　　情况

　　　　解放　　　　　　　　感情

　　　　追求　　　　　　　　自由

（2）　　幸福　　　　　　　　恋爱

　　　　保守　　　　　　　　地位

　　　　社会　　　　　　　　观念

　　　　自由　　　　　　　　家庭

二、选词填空：

　　　　不管......都

　　　　即使......也

　　　　不能......更不能

1 · 孩子_____没有双亲的照顾，_____没有母爱。

2 · _____父母同意不同意，我_____要跟他结婚。

3 · _____你的试验失败了，_____不要灰心。

4 · _____下雨，这场比赛_____要进行。

5 · _____今年能不能得到奖学金，我_____得去中国学习。

6·考试的时候，你_____抄书，_____看别人的试卷。

三、仿照例句，用所给句式或词造句：

（一）用......方式+V

例句：老师用听写的方式，检验学生的学习情况。

1·_____。

2·_____。

（二）再也不用+V

例句：有了电灯以后，人们再也不用点油灯来照明了。

1·_____。

2·_____。

四、造句：

1·由......决定

2·只能

3·受到......限制

4·得到

5·终于

五、仿照例句，用"一直"改写下列句子：

例：中国人的恋爱、婚姻始终受到很多限制。

➜中国人的恋爱、婚姻一直受到很多限制。

1·我昨天在车站等他，车开了，他也没来。

2·我每天学中文，从早上九点到下午三点。

3·他找了很长时间的工作，还没找到。

4·从电影开始到结束，他都在吃玉米花。

5·你往前走，别拐弯。

六、完成句子：

1·从_____我就不抽烟了。

2·不管你有没有钱，_____。

3·_____，我仍然听不懂他说的话。

4·_____，我们只能坐火车去旅行。

5·_____，于是我去找警察。

6·_____，我终于可以去中国了。

7·随着汽车的增多，_____。

8·进入二十一世纪以后，_____。

七、用课文中相应的词或词组将下列句子译成中文：

1. For several thousand years in feudal China, a married couple could not divorce even if they did not love each other.

2. Today's young people in China can hardly believe that fifty years ago, a young person's marriage was not decided by himself, but by his parents.

3. Many sad things happened in feudal China because of the role that social status played in marriage. For instance, the daughter of a wealthy family could not marry the son of a poor man.

4. The "stability" of the family in feudal China was often maintained at the cost of an individual person's interests and feelings.

5. Since the mid-twentieth century, young people in China began to enjoy the freedom of love and the right to make decisions for their own marriages.

6. After the economic reform in China, many people began to seek their own happiness and love bravely. In other words, fundamental changes have eventually taken place in Chinese people's thoughts about marriage.

7. In China today, sometimes when one is looking for a marriage prospect, he or she still pays close attention to the other person's social position.

8. A divorce or second marriage, no longer seen as abnormal in China, is now seldom opposed by children or other members of the family.

9. Despite apparent social progress, there are still some people who try to suppress their true feelings in different ways, because they fear being laughed at by others.

10. It can be said that traditional ideas concerning marriage are still in widespread existence; even some young people have such ideas.

八、想一想，说一说：

1·你曾经笑话过别人吗？你曾经被别人笑话过吗？

2·在你的国家或民族，人们做什么事时，会被别人看不起？

九、写文章：

在你的国家或地区，现在的年青人的恋爱观是否跟父母辈有所不同？有哪些不同之处？为什么？写一篇短文谈谈这几个问题。

3・戀愛　婚姻

一、劃線組詞：

（1）

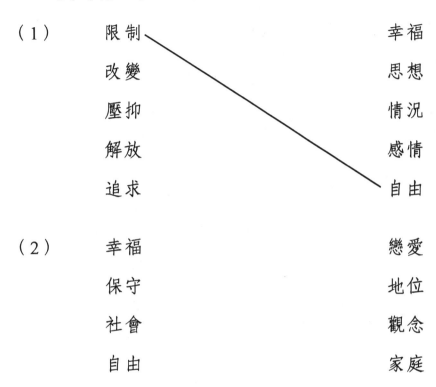

限制　　　　　　　　幸福

改變　　　　　　　　思想

壓抑　　　　　　　　情況

解放　　　　　　　　感情

追求　　　　　　　　自由

（2）

幸福　　　　　　　　戀愛

保守　　　　　　　　地位

社會　　　　　　　　觀念

自由　　　　　　　　家庭

二、選詞填空：

不管......都

即使......也

不能......更不能

1・孩子_____沒有雙親的照顧，_____沒有母愛。

2・_____父母同意不同意，我_____要跟他結婚。

3・_____你的試驗失敗了，_____不要灰心。

4・_____下雨，這場比賽_____要進行。

5・_____今年能不能得到獎學金，我_____得去中國學習。

6‧考試的時候，你_____抄書，_____看別人的試卷。

三、仿照例句，用所給句式或詞造句：

（一）用……方式＋V

例句：老師用聽寫的方式，檢驗學生的學習情況。

1‧_____。

2‧_____。

（二）再也不用＋V

例句：有了電燈以后，人們再也不用點油燈來照明了。

1‧_____。

2‧_____。

四、造句：

1‧由……決定

2‧只能

3‧受到……限制

4‧得到

5‧終於

五、仿照例句，用"一直"改寫下列句子：

例：中國人的戀愛、婚姻始終受到很多限制。

→中國人的戀愛、婚姻一直受到很多限制。

1‧我昨天在車站等他，車開了，他也沒來。

2·我每天學中文，從早上九點到下午三點。

3·他找了很長時間的工作，還沒找到。

4·從電影開始到結束，他都在吃玉米花。

5·你往前走，別拐彎。

六、完成句子：

1·從_____我就不抽煙了。

2·不管你有沒有錢，_____。

3·_____，我仍然聽不懂他說的話。

4·_____，我們只能坐火車去旅行。

5·_____，於是我去找警察。

6·_____，我終於可以去中國了。

7·隨著汽車的增多，_____。

8·進入二十一世紀以后，_____。

七、用課文中相應的詞或詞組將下列句子譯成中文：

1. For several thousand years in feudal China, a married couple could not divorce even if they did not love each other.

2. Today's young people in China can hardly believe that fifty years ago, a young person's marriage was not decided by himself, but by his parents.

3. Many sad things happened in feudal China because of the role that social status played in marriage. For instance, the daughter of a wealthy family could not marry the son of a poor man.

4. The "stability" of the family in feudal China was often maintained at the cost of an individual person's interests and feelings.

5. Since the mid-twentieth century, young people in China began to enjoy the freedom of love and the right to make decisions for their own marriages.

6. After the economic reform in China, many people began to seek their own happiness and love bravely. In other words, fundamental changes have eventually taken place in Chinese people's thoughts about marriage.

7. In China today, sometimes when one is looking for a marriage prospect, he or she still pays close attention to the other person's social position.

8. A divorce or second marriage, no longer seen as abnormal in China, is now seldom opposed by children or other members of the family.

9. Despite apparent social progress, there are still some people who try to suppress their true feelings in different ways, because they fear being laughed at by others.

10. It can be said that traditional ideas concerning marriage are still in widespread existence; even some young people have such ideas.

八、想一想，説一説：

1・你曾經笑話過別人嗎？你曾經被別人笑話過嗎？

2・在你的國家或民族，人們做什麼事時，會被別人看不起？

九、寫文章：

在你的國家或地區，現在的年青人的戀愛觀是否跟父母輩有所不同？有哪些不同之處？為什麼？寫一篇短文談談這幾個問題。

3·1 一则征婚启事和应征者

一、组成动宾词组：

例：介绍---情况

感到---   度过---

具有---   显示---

出现---   追求---

二、仿照例句，用所给句式或词完成句子：

（一）才......就......

例句：才十月，就下雪了。

1·他才学了两个月汉语，_____。

2·他和那个姑娘才见过一面，_____。

3·那个孩子才十岁，_____。

4·我们搬到这里才半年，_____。

（二）是.....来+V+的

例句：是他的老师推荐他来申请这个工作的。

1·是中国美丽的风景吸引我_____。

2·是他妈妈让他_____。

3·是他的朋友帮助他_____。

4·是人类对自然界的无知和幻想，促使人们_____。

（三）......但更重要的是......

例句：我喜欢那个姑娘，因为她长得漂亮，但更重要的是，她具有社交能力。

1·学习中文时，了解中文的语法是很重要的，＿＿＿＿＿＿＿＿＿＿＿＿＿。

2·买车的时候，要考虑汽车的样子，＿＿＿＿＿＿＿＿＿＿＿＿＿＿＿。

3·选择专业要看今后能不能找到工作，＿＿＿＿＿＿＿＿＿＿＿＿＿。

4·我租这套房子，是因为价钱便宜，＿＿＿＿＿＿＿＿＿＿＿＿＿＿。

（四）不是......吗？

例句：那不是你最喜欢的电影明星吗？快去和她一起照相吧！

1·你不是没有钱吗？＿＿＿＿＿＿＿＿＿＿＿＿＿＿＿＿＿＿＿。

2·你不是想学中文吗？＿＿＿＿＿＿＿＿＿＿＿＿＿＿＿＿＿＿。

3·他不是中国人吗？＿＿＿＿＿＿＿＿＿＿＿＿＿＿＿＿＿＿＿。

4·电影票不是卖完了吗？＿＿＿＿＿＿＿＿＿＿＿＿＿＿＿＿＿。

三、完成句子：

1·打了一个雷，接着＿＿＿＿＿＿＿＿＿＿＿＿＿＿＿＿＿＿＿＿。

2·他唱完了歌，接着＿＿＿＿＿＿＿＿＿＿＿＿＿＿＿＿＿＿＿＿。

3·这个公司用优越的经济条件来＿＿＿＿＿＿＿＿＿＿＿＿＿＿＿。

4·你父母这么关心你，你得好好学习来＿＿＿＿＿＿＿＿＿＿＿＿。

5·他拿了五百元钱去＿＿＿＿＿＿＿＿＿＿＿＿＿＿＿＿＿＿＿＿。

6·你要来这个公司工作就必须具有＿＿＿＿＿＿＿＿＿＿＿＿＿＿。

7·我爱他，因为他具有＿＿＿＿＿＿＿＿＿＿＿＿＿＿＿＿＿＿＿。

8·在这个班里，百分之八十以上的学生＿＿＿＿＿＿＿＿＿＿＿＿。

9·＿＿＿＿＿＿＿＿＿＿＿＿＿＿＿＿＿＿＿＿＿＿在五千元以上。

四、造句：

1 · 痛快

2 · 其实

3 · 对......感兴趣

4 · 有所作为

5 · 机会

6 · 实践

五、用所给词，说说在报纸上或电视上征婚的过程：

　　　希望　　　具有　　　吸引　　　显示　　　先......接着

　　　追求　　　终于　　　条件　　　机会　　　满意

六、看图，用"正在......中"编写句子：

1 · 球赛_____。

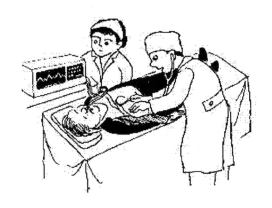

2·病人_____。

3·木头_____。

4·汽车_____。

5·他们_____。

七、用所给词语将下列句子译成中文：

1. This company is going to hire a PR manager. The ideal candidate should know how to use the computer, can speak Japanese, and has an education beyond high school. （具有......水平）

2. This joint-venture is known for its competitive salary and excellent benefits. That is why it has attracted so many job-seekers. （吸引）

nà shì weishenme xiyin néng cào qiú zhi zhě de yuányin.

93

3. The first girl to respond to the advertisement was a college graduate. She said that she was attracted by the superior financial position of the young entrepreneur. （吸引）

4. Last Saturday, I had invited only five friends to my birthday party. However, more than thirty people showed up unexpectedly. （没想到）

5. All his relatives in his home town in China think he has made a fortune in America. As a matter of fact, he is a janitor in an apartment building in New York. （其实）

6. My cousin had an accident last week. Fortunately, she was not injured, but her car was badly damaged and is being repaired.
（正在......中）

7. His success in this international piano competition is certainly due to the excellent instruction of his teacher. More importantly, he has made a far greater effort than anybody else. （更重要的是）

8. As soon as the delegates walked out of the conference room, journalists surrounded them and asked them a lot of questions about the results of the negotiation. （向......提问题）

9. It has been recognized by historians that President Nixon's（尼克松）
   visit to China in 1972 is of great historical significance.
   （具有......意义）

10. After the multicultural festival（多元文化节）, the president of the
    university sent the student organizers a congratulatory note, in which the
    president stressed that this event showed these students' leadership abilities.
    （显示......才能）

八、读副课文，回答问题：

1·你认为"电话红娘"、"电视征婚"这些方法好吗？

2·在你的国家和民族，人们喜欢采用这些征婚方式吗？

3·你认为如果不愿意去电视上征婚，就是"受旧的传统观念影响"吗？

九、想一想，说一说：

1·你有哪些"特别"的能力？

2·你对中国文化的哪些方面感兴趣？

3·业余生活中，什么最能吸引你？

4·你认为什么叫"有所作为"？

5·你喜欢"平平淡淡"的生活，还是"冒险"的生活？

3·1　　一則征婚啓事和應征者

一、組成動賓詞組：

例：介紹---情況

感到---　　　　　　　　　　　　度過---

具有---　　　　　　　　　　　　顯示---

出現---　　　　　　　　　　　　追求---

二、仿照例句，用所給句式或詞完成句子：

（一）才......就......

例句：<u>才</u>十月，<u>就</u>下雪了。

1·他才學了兩個月漢語，＿＿＿＿＿＿＿＿＿＿＿＿＿＿＿＿。

2·他和那個姑娘才見過一面，＿＿＿＿＿＿＿＿＿＿＿＿＿＿。

3·那個孩子才十歲，＿＿＿＿＿＿＿＿＿＿＿＿＿＿＿＿＿。

4·我們搬到這里才半年，＿＿＿＿＿＿＿＿＿＿＿＿＿＿＿。

（二）是.....來+V+的

例句：<u>是</u>他的老師推薦他<u>來</u>申請這個工作<u>的</u>。

1·是中國美麗的風景吸引我＿＿＿＿＿＿＿＿＿＿＿＿＿＿＿。

2·是他媽媽讓他＿＿＿＿＿＿＿＿＿＿＿＿＿＿＿＿＿＿＿。

3·是他的朋友幫助他＿＿＿＿＿＿＿＿＿＿＿＿＿＿＿＿＿。

4·是人類對自然界的無知和幻想，促使人們＿＿＿＿＿＿＿＿。

（三）......但更重要的是......

例句：我喜歡那個姑娘，因為她長得漂亮，<u>但更重要的是</u>，她具有社交能力。

1 · 學習中文時，了解中文的語法是很重要的，_____。

2 · 買車的時候，要考慮汽車的樣子，_____。

3 · 選擇專業要看今後能不能找到工作，_____。

4 · 我租這套房子，是因為價錢便宜，_____。

（四）不是......嗎？

例句：那<u>不是</u>你最喜歡的電影明星<u>嗎</u>？快去和她一起照相吧！

1 · 你不是沒有錢嗎？_____。

2 · 你不是想學中文嗎？_____。

3 · 他不是中國人嗎？_____。

4 · 電影票不是賣完了嗎？_____。

三、完成句子：

1 · 打了一個雷，接著_____。

2 · 他唱完了歌，接著_____。

3 · 這個公司用優越的經濟條件來_____。

4 · 你父母這麼關心你，你得好好學習來_____。

5 · 他拿了五百元錢去_____。

6 · 你要來這個公司工作就必須具有_____。

7 · 我愛他，因為他具有_____。

8 · 在這個班里，百分之八十以上的學生_____。

9 · _____在五千元以上。

四、造句：

1・痛快

2・其實

3・對......感興趣

4・有所作為

5・機會

6・實踐

五、用所給詞，説説在報紙上或電視上征婚的過程：

希望　　　具有　　　吸引　　　顯示　　　先......接著

追求　　　終於　　　條件　　　機會　　　滿意

六、看圖，用“正在......中”編寫句子：

1・球賽_____。

2・病人_____。

3・木頭_____。

4・汽車_____。

5・他們_____。

七、用所給詞語將下列句子譯成中文：

1. This company is going to hire a PR manager. The ideal candidate should know how to use the computer, can speak Japanese, and has an education beyond high school. （具有......水平）

2. This joint-venture is known for its competitive salary and excellent benefits. That is why it has attracted so many job-seekers. （吸引）

3. The first girl to respond to the advertisement was a college graduate. She said that she was attracted by the superior financial position of the young entrepreneur. （吸引）

4. Last Saturday, I had invited only five friends to my birthday party. However, more than thirty people showed up unexpectedly. （沒想到）

5. All his relatives in his home town in China think he has made a fortune in America. As a matter of fact, he is a janitor in an apartment building in New York. （其實）

6. My cousin had an accident last week. Fortunately, she was not injured, but her car was badly damaged and is being repaired.
（正在......中）

7. His success in this international piano competition is certainly due to the excellent instruction of his teacher. More importantly, he has made a far greater effort than anybody else. （更重要的是）

8. As soon as the delegates walked out of the conference room, journalists surrounded them and asked them a lot of questions about the results of the negotiation. （向......提問題）

9. It has been recognized by historians that President Nixon's（尼克松）
   visit to China in 1972 is of great historical significance.
   （具有......意義）

10. After the multicultural festival（多元文化節）, the president of the
    university sent the student organizers a congratulatory note, in which the
    president stressed that this event showed these students' leadership abilities.
    （顯示......才能）

八、讀副課文，回答問題：

1．你認為"電話紅娘"、"電視征婚"這些方法好嗎？

2．在你的國家和民族，人們喜歡采用這些征婚方式嗎？

3．你認為如果不願意去電視上征婚，就是"受舊的傳統觀念影響"嗎？

九、想一想，說一說：

1．你有哪些"特別"的能力？

2．你對中國文化的哪些方面感興趣？

3．業余生活中，什麼最能吸引你？

4．你認為什麼叫"有所作為"？

5．你喜歡"平平淡淡"的生活，還是"冒險"的生活？

3 · 2　黄昏之恋

一、组成动宾词组：

例：发展 - - - 经济

指挥 - - -　　　　　　　　　表演 - - -

说明 - - -　　　　　　　　　赞成 - - -

反对 - - -　　　　　　　　　收拾 - - -

二、完成下列句子：

1·今天我很早就起床了，谁知道，＿＿＿＿＿＿＿＿＿＿＿＿＿＿。

2·这次考试以前，我复习了很长时间，谁知道，＿＿＿＿＿＿＿。

3·我的车坏了，我只好＿＿＿＿＿＿＿＿＿＿＿＿＿＿＿＿＿。

4·他没有钱，只好＿＿＿＿＿＿＿＿＿＿＿＿＿＿＿＿＿＿。

5·既然我们是朋友，＿＿＿＿＿＿＿＿＿＿＿＿＿＿＿＿＿。

6·既然天下雨，＿＿＿＿＿＿＿＿＿＿＿＿＿＿＿＿＿＿＿。

7·我的书找不到了，原来＿＿＿＿＿＿＿＿＿＿＿＿＿＿＿。

8·他们俩长得很像，原来＿＿＿＿＿＿＿＿＿＿＿＿＿＿＿。

三、给下列句子中划线的词注音，并仿照例句造句：

1·爷爷一听可<u>着</u>了急。

2·他只好带<u>着</u>聪聪一起到"她"那里去。

3·屋前还<u>种</u>着各<u>种</u>好看的花。

4·爷爷走了，谁<u>看</u>聪聪。

5·小俩口先对<u>看</u>一下。

四、选词填空：

  既然   猛然   不自然   虽然

1·他在朋友家又遇到了他的前妻，他觉得很_____。

2·_____他已经三十岁了，但是他还靠父母养活。

3·_____跳出一条狗来，把他吓了一跳。

4·_____你爱他，就和他结婚吧！

五、仿照例句，用划线的词造句：

1·爷爷一听<u>可</u>着了急。

2·儿子媳妇在家，不好意思出来，<u>可</u>心里老想着你。

3·儿子<u>一</u>听<u>就</u>觉得别扭。

4·<u>都怪你</u>，自己不送孩子，一定要那么早去上班，现在<u>可好</u>，老爷子送孙子<u>连</u>自己<u>都</u>送丢了。

5·<u>想当年</u>，自己能指挥一个团，<u>现在</u>却连一个五岁的孩子都指挥不了。

6·聪聪<u>边</u>走<u>边</u>唱，高兴极了。

六、分辨两个句子中划线词在词义上的异同，并分别造句：

（一）

1·小俩口先对看了一下，<u>然后</u>一起看着老爷子。

2·她介绍了自己，<u>接着</u>又向征婚者提了许多问题。

（二）

1·<u>既然</u>聪聪来了，<u>就</u>一分为二，让他和聪聪各吃半碗。

2·<u>因为</u>遇到一个好奶奶，<u>所以</u>聪聪一定要玩到吃完晚饭才走。

（三）

1·儿子一听就觉得别扭，可又很难反对，<u>于是</u>看了看妻子。

2·你的条件优越，一定会有许多姑娘来应征，<u>所以</u>我就想出来这个主意。

七、造句：

1·要是

2·倒是

3·从来不

4·从来没......过

八、用所给词语将下列句子译成中文：

1. He suddenly woke up from his dream, and discovered that the house was on fire. （猛然）

2. I can't believe that you cannot answer this question. It is so simple that even a seven-year-old child can answer it. （连......都......）

3. This semester, I am taking six courses, including Chinese history and business writing. I am so busy that I don't even have time to wash my dirty clothes. （连......都......）

4. Xiao Zhang told his father that he was admitted into the business school of Beijing University. His father was very glad after hearing this news. （可＋Adj＋了）

5. This year my younger sister's roommate is a freshman student from Japan. They get along with each other so well that they want to be roommates again next year. （合得来）

6. Before students started working on the exam, the teacher asked them to pay attention to questions on grammar and clearly explained to the students his requirements. （说明）

7. Don't worry. We are not going to that seafood restaurant for dinner since you don't like to eat fish. （既然......就......）

8. The young man is a brilliant writer, but not a good speaker. He feels awkward whenever he has to talk in front of many people. （觉得别扭）

9. She would never change her view just because other people are not pleased with it. （从来＋不／没）

10. I don't need this Chinese-English dictionary because I already have one. But it would be a good birthday gift if you give it to my younger brother. （倒是）

九、读副课文，选择正确答案：

1．王路中想找一个伴侣，因为他

    A：退休了   B：最近离婚了

    C：太忙，没时间做家务   D：孤独

2．应征者中有一封广州姑娘的来信最吸引他，因为

    A：女儿替妈妈找对象   B：她的经济条件最好

    C：从照片上看，她很漂亮   D：她的住房条件不错

3．妈妈自己不应征，是因为

      A：她爱女儿　　　　　　　　B：她不好意思

      C：除了母女情，她不需要别的感情　D：她的生活很幸福

4．妈妈知道女儿为她应征后，感到

      A：很生气　　　　　　　　　　B：很害羞

      C：很感动　　　　　　　　　　D：很不好意思

十、想一想，说一说：

1．你知道为什么在中国一些子女干扰、反对老年人的恋爱和婚姻吗？

2．在你的国家或民族，人们如何对待老年人的恋爱和婚姻？

3·2　黄昏之戀

一、組成動賓詞組：

例：發展---經濟

指揮---　　　　　　　　　表演---

説明---　　　　　　　　　贊成---

反對---　　　　　　　　　收拾---

二、完成下列句子：

1·今天我很早就起床了，誰知道，＿＿＿＿＿＿＿＿＿＿＿＿＿＿＿。

2·這次考試以前，我復習了很長時間，誰知道，＿＿＿＿＿＿＿。

3·我的車壞了，我只好＿＿＿＿＿＿＿＿＿＿＿＿＿＿＿＿。

4·他沒有錢，只好＿＿＿＿＿＿＿＿＿＿＿＿＿＿＿＿＿＿。

5·既然我們是朋友，＿＿＿＿＿＿＿＿＿＿＿＿＿＿＿＿＿。

6·既然天下雨，＿＿＿＿＿＿＿＿＿＿＿＿＿＿＿＿＿＿＿。

7·我的書找不到了，原來＿＿＿＿＿＿＿＿＿＿＿＿＿＿＿＿。

8·他們倆長得很像，原來＿＿＿＿＿＿＿＿＿＿＿＿＿＿＿＿。

三、給下列句子中劃線的詞注音，並仿照例句造句：

1·爺爺一聽可<u>著</u>了急。

2·他只好帶<u>著</u>聰聰一起到"她"那里去。

3·屋前還<u>種</u>著各<u>種</u>好看的花。

4·爺爺走了，誰<u>看</u>聰聰。

5・小倆口先對<u>看</u>一下。

四、選詞填空：

既然　　　猛然　　　不自然　　　雖然

1・他在朋友家又遇到了他的前妻，他覺得很＿＿＿＿＿＿＿＿＿＿。

2・＿＿＿＿＿＿＿＿＿＿＿他已經三十歲了，但是他還靠父母養活。

3・＿＿＿＿＿＿＿＿＿＿＿跳出一條狗來，把他嚇了一跳。

4・＿＿＿＿＿＿＿＿＿＿你愛他，就和他結婚吧！

五、仿照例句，用劃線的詞造句：

1・爺爺一聽<u>可</u>著了急。

2・兒子媳婦在家，不好意思出來，<u>可</u>心里老想著你。

3・兒子<u>一</u>聽<u>就</u>覺得別扭。

4・<u>都怪你</u>，自己不送孩子，一定要那麼早去上班，現在<u>可好</u>，老爺子

送孫子<u>連</u>自己<u>都</u>送丟了。

5・<u>想當年</u>，自己能指揮一個團，<u>現在</u>卻連一個五歲的孩子都指揮不

了。

6・聰聰<u>邊</u>走<u>邊</u>唱，高興極了。

六、分辨兩個句子中劃線詞在詞義上的異同，並分別造句：

（一）

1・小倆口先對看了一下，<u>然後</u>一起看著老爺子。

2・她介紹了自己，<u>接著</u>又向征婚者提了許多問題。

（二）

1 · <u>既然</u>聰聰來了，<u>就</u>一分為二，讓他和聰聰各吃半碗。

2 · <u>因為</u>遇到一個好奶奶，<u>所以</u>聰聰一定要玩到吃完晚飯才走。

（三）

1 · 兒子一聽就覺得別扭，可又很難反對，<u>於是</u>看了看妻子。

2 · 你的條件優越，一定會有許多姑娘來應征，<u>所以</u>我就想出來這個主意。

七、造句：

1 · 要是

2 · 倒是

3 · 從來不

4 · 從來沒......過

八、用所給詞語將下列句子譯成中文：

1. He suddenly woke up from his dream, and discovered that the house was on fire. （猛然）

2. I can't believe that you cannot answer this question. It is so simple that even a seven-year-old child can answer it. （連......都......）

3. This semester, I am taking six courses, including Chinese history and business writing. I am so busy that I don't even have time to wash my dirty clothes. （連......都......）

4. Xiao Zhang told his father that he was admitted into the business school of Beijing University. His father was very glad after hearing this news. （可＋Adj＋了）

5. This year my younger sister's roommate is a freshman student from Japan. They get along with each other so well that they want to be roommates again next year. （合得來）

6. Before students started working on the exam, the teacher asked them to pay attention to questions on grammar and clearly explained to the students his requirements. （說明）

7. Don't worry. We are not going to that seafood restaurant for dinner since you don't like to eat fish. （既然......就......）

8. The young man is a brilliant writer, but not a good speaker. He feels awkward whenever he has to talk in front of many people. （覺得別扭）

9. She would never change her view just because other people are not pleased with it. （從來＋不／沒）

10. I don't need this Chinese-English dictionary because I already have one. But it would be a good birthday gift if you give it to my younger brother. （倒是）

九、讀副課文，選擇正確答案：

1・王路中想找一個伴侶，因為他

    A：退休了   B：最近離婚了

    C：太忙，沒時間做家務   D：孤獨

2・應征者中有一封廣州姑娘的來信最吸引他，因為

    A：女兒替媽媽找對象   B：她的經濟條件最好

    C：從照片上看，她很漂亮   D：她的住房條件不錯

3．媽媽自己不應征，是因為

      A：她愛女兒　　　　　　　　B：她不好意思

      C：除了母女情，她不需要別的感情　　D：她的生活很幸福

4．媽媽知道女兒為她應征後，感到

      A：很生氣　　　　　　　　　B：很害羞

      C：很感動　　　　　　　　　D：很不好意思

十、想一想，說一說：

1．你知道為什麼在中國一些子女干擾、反對老年人的戀愛和婚姻嗎？

2．在你的國家或民族，人們如何對待老年人的戀愛和婚姻？

3·3　中国婚姻观念变化的新现象：
公证婚前财产协议

一、用中文解释下列词语：

婚姻观	一穷二白	咨询	财产公证
不动产	热门话题	白领	市场经济

二、组成动宾词组：

例：解决－－－问题

拥有－－－　　　　　　　　　　　　处理－－－

避免－－－　　　　　　　　　　　　承担－－－

影响－－－　　　　　　　　　　　　看管－－－

三、仿照例句，用所给的句式或词造句：

（一）从……变为……

例句：中国的经济体制已<u>从</u>计划经济<u>变为</u>了市场经济。

1·_____。

2·_____。

（二）随着……而……

例句：在中国，住房问题<u>随着</u>人口的增加<u>而</u>变得越来越严重了。

1·_____。

2·_____。

（三）要想……得先……

例句：你<u>要</u>想去中国工作，<u>得</u>先学会说中文。

1．＿＿＿＿＿＿＿＿＿＿＿＿＿＿＿＿＿＿＿＿＿＿＿＿＿＿＿＿＿＿＿。

2．＿＿＿＿＿＿＿＿＿＿＿＿＿＿＿＿＿＿＿＿＿＿＿＿＿＿＿＿＿＿＿。

四、造句：

1．于是

2．怀疑

3．逐渐

4．相当

5．借口

五、完成句子：

1．你要想考试成绩好，就得＿＿＿＿＿＿＿＿＿＿＿＿＿＿＿＿＿＿＿。

2．这件事很复杂，牵扯＿＿＿＿＿＿＿＿＿＿＿＿＿＿＿＿＿＿＿＿＿。

3．要想婚姻美满，有人主张＿＿＿＿＿＿＿＿＿＿＿＿＿＿＿＿＿＿。

4．他开车总是开得很快，造成＿＿＿＿＿＿＿＿＿＿＿＿＿＿＿＿＿。

5．这辆汽车性能很好，值得＿＿＿＿＿＿＿＿＿＿＿＿＿＿＿＿＿＿。

6．不要开快车，避免＿＿＿＿＿＿＿＿＿＿＿＿＿＿＿＿＿＿＿＿＿。

7．你的学习成绩不好，证明＿＿＿＿＿＿＿＿＿＿＿＿＿＿＿＿＿＿。

8．我们很多年没见面了，我几乎＿＿＿＿＿＿＿＿＿＿＿＿＿＿＿＿。

9．据我所知，＿＿＿＿＿＿＿＿＿＿＿＿＿＿＿＿＿＿＿＿＿＿＿＿＿。

六 · 看图说话：

寡母再嫁之前

七、用所给词语将下列句子译成中文：

1. My grandma used to have a very good memory. But now, as she is
   getting old, her memory is becoming poor.
   （随着......而......）

2. Mismanagement and poor marketing strategies have caused such
   damaging losses for this company that it has to file for bankruptcy.
   （造成）

3. After going through many ups and downs in the war, in 1946 we finally
   settled down in a small town and owned our first home. （拥有）

4. According to investigations, the suspect was a male in his early thirties, wearing a black T-shirt and blue jeans, and driving a new white Camry. （据调查）

5. This Chinese automobile company has decided to design this year's new model to attract middle-aged consumers, because they form a considerably large portion of new-car buyers. （占......比例）

6. Because she has been cheated many times, the old lady no longer trusts others. Even when people offer to help her, she suspects their intentions. （怀疑）

7. If you expect to have a successful spring picnic with a good turnout, you should first have a good plan. （要想......得先......）

8. The city government is planning to build a lot of new residential houses in this district. Since this new development plan concerns the benefits of many people, the mayor wants to hold a meeting to collect opinions from community representatives. （牵扯到）

9. The Chinese movie last weekend on campus drew a huge audience. That is a reflection of students' strong interest in Chinese culture. （反映）

10. Xi'an is an ancient capital and full of historical attractions. It is really worth visiting. （值得）

八、读副课文，回答问题：

1．一般中国人关于人生道路的传统观念是什么？

2．"男大当婚，女大当嫁"是什么意思？

3．有哪几种现代女性不愿意结婚？

4．你怎样看待第一种独身女性？

5．你觉得第二种独身女性的想法是否实际？

6．独身主义是一种社会进步的现象吗？

九、想一想，说一说：

1．你认为"公证"是中国婚姻制度上的一个历史性的进步吗？为什么？

2．你能接受公证婚前财产协议这种作法吗？

3．在你的国家或民族，人们在结婚时，是如何处理婚前财产的？

3・3　中國婚姻觀念變化的新現象：
公證婚前財產協議

一、用中文解釋下列詞語：

婚姻觀	一窮二白	咨詢	財產公證
不動產	熱門話題	白領	市場經濟

二、組成動賓詞組：

例：解決---問題

擁有---　　　　　　　　　　　處理---

避免---　　　　　　　　　　　承擔---

影響---　　　　　　　　　　　看管---

三、仿照例句，用所給的句式或詞造句：

（一）從......變為......

例句：中國的經濟體制已從計劃經濟變為了市場經濟。

1.＿＿＿＿＿＿＿＿＿＿＿＿＿＿＿＿＿＿＿＿＿＿＿＿＿＿＿＿＿。

2.＿＿＿＿＿＿＿＿＿＿＿＿＿＿＿＿＿＿＿＿＿＿＿＿＿＿＿＿＿。

（二）隨著......而......

例句：在中國，住房問題隨著人口的增加而變得越來越嚴重了。

1.＿＿＿＿＿＿＿＿＿＿＿＿＿＿＿＿＿＿＿＿＿＿＿＿＿＿＿＿＿。

2.＿＿＿＿＿＿＿＿＿＿＿＿＿＿＿＿＿＿＿＿＿＿＿＿＿＿＿＿＿。

（三）要想......得先......

例句：你<u>要想</u>去中國工作，<u>得先</u>學會說中文。

1. _____。

2. _____。

四、造句：

1. 於是

2. 懷疑

3. 逐漸

4. 相當

5. 借口

五、完成句子：

1. 你要想考試成績好，就得_____。

2. 這件事很復雜，牽扯_____。

3. 要想婚姻美滿，有人主張_____。

4. 他開車總是開得很快，造成_____。

5. 這輛汽車性能很好，值得_____。

6. 不要開快車，避免_____。

7. 你的學習成績不好，證明_____。

8. 我們很多年沒見面了，我幾乎_____。

9. 據我所知，_____。

六‧看圖說話：

寡母再嫁之前

七、用所給詞語將下列句子譯成中文：

1. My grandma used to have a very good memory. But now, as she is
   getting old, her memory is becoming poor.
   （隨著……而……）

2. Mismanagement and poor marketing strategies have caused such
   damaging losses for this company that it has to file for bankruptcy.
   （造成）

3. After going through many ups and downs in the war, in 1946 we finally
   settled down in a small town and owned our first home.（擁有）

4. According to investigations, the suspect was a male in his early thirties, wearing a black T-shirt and blue jeans, and driving a new white Camry. （據調查）

5. This Chinese automobile company has decided to design this year's new model to attract middle-aged consumers, because they form a considerably large portion of new-car buyers. （佔......比例）

6. Because she has been cheated many times, the old lady no longer trusts others. Even when people offer to help her, she suspects their intentions. （懷疑）

7. If you expect to have a successful spring picnic with a good turnout, you should first have a good plan. （要想......得先......）

8. The city government is planning to build a lot of new residential houses in this district. Since this new development plan concerns the benefits of many people, the mayor wants to hold a meeting to collect opinions from community representatives. （牽扯到）

9. The Chinese movie last weekend on campus drew a huge audience. That is a reflection of students' strong interest in Chinese culture. （反映）

10. Xi'an is an ancient capital and full of historical attractions. It is really worth visiting. （值得）

八、讀副課文，回答問題：

1．一般中國人關于人生道路的傳統觀念是什麼？

2．"男大當婚，女大當嫁"是什麼意思？

3．有哪幾種現代女性不願意結婚？

4．你怎樣看待第一種獨身女性？

5．你覺得第二種獨身女性的想法是否實際？

6．獨身主義是一種社會進步的現象嗎？

九、想一想，説一説：

1．你認為"公證"是中國婚姻制度上的一個歷史性的進步嗎？為什麼？

2．你能接受公證婚前財產協議這種作法嗎？

3．在你的國家或民族，人們在結婚時，是如何處理婚前財產的？

4. 家庭　妇女　儿童

一、划线，组成动宾词组：

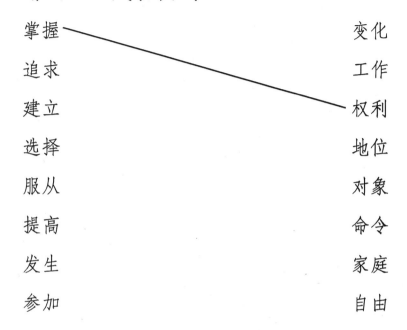

掌握　　　　　　　　　　变化
追求　　　　　　　　　　工作
建立　　　　　　　　　　权利
选择　　　　　　　　　　地位
服从　　　　　　　　　　对象
提高　　　　　　　　　　命令
发生　　　　　　　　　　家庭
参加　　　　　　　　　　自由

二、填上适当的字，组成动宾词组：

（　　）立家庭　　　　　（　　）护利益

（　　）立榜样　　　　　（　　）护公物

成（　　）公司　　　　　（　　）护儿童

三、区分下列几组句子中划线词语的不同意思，并仿照例句造句：

（一）

1．这种心理状态<u>自然</u>会影响到婚姻的美满。

2．避免环境污染，保护<u>自然</u>环境。

125

（二）

1 · 要想婚后生活安宁，得先在婚前<u>处理</u>好各自的财产。

2 · 那些商品是<u>处理</u>的。

（三）

1 · 结婚后不幸福也不愿意离婚，怕别人<u>笑话</u>、瞧不起。

2 · 他说的那个<u>笑话</u>真可笑。

（四）

1 · 家长不再有那么大的<u>权力</u>了。

2 · 投票选举总统是每一个公民的<u>权利</u>。

四、完成句子：

1 · 他没有钱买房子，只能_____。

2 · 去那个地方，没有飞机和火车，我只能_____。

3 · 这次考试，他考得不好，几乎_____。

4 · 这几天我忙极了，几乎_____。

5 · 这里不再是公园，而是_____。

6 · 她不再是秘书，而是_____。

7 · 他不再喝咖啡，而_____。

8 · 我们不再学法文，而_____。

9 · 哪个学生学习努力，_____就_____。

10 · 哪本书有意思，_____就_____。

11 · 我不知道他住在哪儿，甚至_____。

12 · 他很穷，没有房子住，甚至_____。

五、造句：

1．掌握

2．当

3．服从

4．维护

5．开始＋V

6．让＋N＋V

六、用所给词语将下列句子译成中文：

1. In many rural areas in China, very often it is still the husband, not the wife, who controls the financial affairs of the family and decides the future of the children.（掌握，决定）

2. The ideal family in traditional China is one with three and even four generations living together. Such a family is now rarely seen in China. Instead, a new family structure is being established.（建立）

3. With the efforts of the leaders of both countries, the People's Republic of China established normal diplomatic relations with the United States in 1978.（建立）

4. In a real democratic country, if the people want the head of their government to step down, then he must step down.
（要......就必须......）

5. The reason why she does not like her own country is that, in that country, whoever possesses money possesses power.
（哪个......哪个......）

6. In an advanced country like the United States, almost every family owns a car. In contrast, in some developing countries, there are people who have never seen a car. （几乎）

7. After he failed the mid-term exams for two classes, my younger brother doesn't watch TV or play computer games any more, but rather focuses on his studies every evening. （不再......而是......）

8. At yesterday's meeting, the guest speaker said that the problem of unemployment does not exist in his country. I don't think he told the truth. （存在）

9. Many politicians are only interested in pursuing power and protecting their own positions. （维护）

10. Because she worked hard and maintained a good relationship with her co-workers in the office, this young woman was promoted to the department manager only two years after graduating from college. （当上了）

七、想一想，说一说：

1·你认为什么样的家庭结构是理想的家庭结构？

2·你的家庭价值观是什么样的？

八、写文章：

　　对你来说，什么样的家庭是比较理想的家庭？这样的家庭应该有什么样的家庭结构？家庭成员之间应该是什么样的关系？你为什么喜欢这样的家庭？围绕这些问题，写一篇约二百字左右的文章，谈谈你的家庭价值观。

4· 家庭　婦女　兒童

一、劃線，組成動賓詞組：

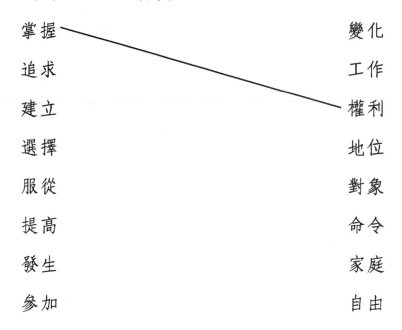

掌握　　　　　　　　變化
追求　　　　　　　　工作
建立　　　　　　　　權利
選擇　　　　　　　　地位
服從　　　　　　　　對象
提高　　　　　　　　命令
發生　　　　　　　　家庭
參加　　　　　　　　自由

二、填上適當的字，組成動賓詞組：

（　　）立家庭　　　　　　　　（　　）護利益

（　　）立榜樣　　　　　　　　（　　）護公物

成（　　）公司　　　　　　　　（　　）護兒童

三、區分下列幾組句子中劃線詞語的不同意思，並仿照例句
　　造句：

（一）

1· 這種心理狀態<u>自然</u>會影響到婚姻的美滿。

2· 避免環境污染，保護<u>自然</u>環境。

（二）

1· 要想婚後生活安寧，得先在婚前 <u>處理</u> 好各自的財產。

2· 那 <u>些</u> 商品是 <u>處理</u> 的。

（三）

1· 結婚後不幸福也不願意離婚，怕別人 <u>笑話</u>、瞧不起。

2· 他說的那個 <u>笑話</u> 真可笑。

（四）

1· 家長不再有那麼大的 <u>權力</u> 了。

2· 投票選舉總統是每一個公民的 <u>權利</u>。

四、完成句子：

1· 他沒有錢買房子，只能_____。

2· 去那個地方，沒有飛機和火車，我只能_____。

3· 這次考試，他考得不好，幾乎_____。

4· 這几天我忙極了，幾乎_____。

5· 這里不再是公園，而是_____。

6· 她不再是秘書，而是_____。

7· 他不再喝咖啡，而_____。

8· 我們不再學法文，而_____。

9· 哪個學生學習努力，_____就_____。

10· 哪本書有意思，_____就_____。

11· 我不知道他住在哪兒，甚至_____。

12· 他很窮，沒有房子住，甚至_____。

五、造句：

1‧掌握

2‧當

3‧服從

4‧維護

5‧開始＋V

6‧讓＋N＋V

六、用所給詞語將下列句子譯成中文：

1. In many rural areas in China, very often it is still the husband, not the wife, who controls the financial affairs of the family and decides the future of the children. （掌握，決定）

2. The ideal family in traditional China is one with three and even four generations living together. Such a family is now rarely seen in China. Instead, a new family structure is being established. （建立）

3. With the efforts of the leaders of both countries, the People's Republic of China established normal diplomatic relations with the United States in 1978. （建立）

4. In a real democratic country, if the people want the head of their government to step down, then he must step down.
（要......就必須......）

5. The reason why she does not like her own country is that, in that country, whoever possesses money possesses power.
（哪個......哪個......）

6. In an advanced country like the United States, almost every family owns a car. In contrast, in some developing countries, there are people who have never seen a car. （幾乎）

7. After he failed the mid-term exams for two classes, my younger brother doesn't watch TV or play computer games any more, but rather focuses on his studies every evening. （不再......而是......）

8. At yesterday's meeting, the guest speaker said that the problem of unemployment does not exist in his country. I don't think he told the truth. （存在）

9. Many politicians are only interested in pursuing power and protecting their own positions.　（維護）

10. Because she worked hard and maintained a good relationship with her co-workers in the office, this young woman was promoted to the department manager only two years after graduating from college. （當上了）

七、想一想，說一說：

1・你認為什麼樣的家庭結構是理想的家庭結構？
2・你的家庭價值觀是什麼樣的？

八、寫文章：

　　對你來說，什麼樣的家庭是比較理想的家庭？這樣的家庭應該有什麼樣的家庭結構？家庭成員之間應該是什麼樣的關系？你為什麼喜歡這樣的家庭？圍繞這些問題，寫一篇約二百字左右的文章，談談你的家庭價值觀。

4·1　我和老伴儿的拳舞之争

一、写出反义词：

表扬---　　　　　　　　　早晨---

轻浮---　　　　　　　　　推辞---

聚---　　　　　　　　　　吵---

二、作出动作，并写出适当的动宾词组：

例：举---举手

挥---　　　　　　　　　　打---

扭---　　　　　　　　　　跳---

拉---　　　　　　　　　　推---

三、区分下列句子中"一"的不同意思，并模仿造句：

1·老伴儿天一亮就往公园跑。

2·打一早晨太极拳还不如我跳五分钟的活动量大。

3·爷爷一喜欢就教她打几路拳。

四、仿照例句，用所给句式或词完成句子：

（一）等......就......

例句：等雨停了，我们就去划船。

1·_____。

2·_____。

（二）当......时，就......

例句：<u>当</u>他拿到工资<u>时</u>，<u>就</u>马上去买新衣服。

1. _____ 。

2. _____ 。

（三）对......来说

例句：人口问题<u>对</u>很多国家<u>来说</u>，都是一大难题。

1. _____ 。

2. _____ 。

五、完成句子：

1. 我们都想吃饺子，他则_____ 。

2. 我喜欢唱歌，我妹妹则_____ 。

3. 昨天他说想去中国，今天则_____ 。

4. 我们坐飞机去旅行吧，省得_____ 。

5. 你赶快复习功课吧，省得_____ 。

6. 给你妈妈打个电话吧，省得_____ 。

7. 这一百块钱的衣服，还不如_____ 。

8. 他不如他弟弟_____ 。

9. 这里的天气不如_____ 。

10. 他既无钱，又无_____ 。

11. _____，可他还是去看电影了。

12. _____，但她还是觉得住在乡下好。

六、造句：

1 · 跟不上

2 · 改行

3 · 欢迎 + N + V

4 · 争论

5 · 推辞

七、用所给词语将下列句子译成中文：

1. In recent years, the number of students applying to teachers' colleges has declined, largely because the profession of teaching is no longer attractive to young people. （近年来）

2. After being a truck driver for five years, he thought he needed to spend more time with his family. So he changed his profession and became a salesman. （改行）

3. Students from the Chinese Department performed a Chinese comedy at the New Year party. The funniest thing of all is that in the comedy, all the male students played the female roles, while all the female students played the male roles. （可笑）

4. The film is a truthful reflection of the suffering of the Chinese people during the Second World War. However, it might be too difficult for American students who have little knowledge of Chinese history. （对......来说）

5. To her surprise, Mrs. Li discovered that lately her son had become obsessed with *kung fu* movies and went to the movie theater after school every day. （迷上了）

6. This little boy told his grandma that after he grew up, he would make a lot of money and buy her a big mansion. The old woman was delighted with his childish promise. （等）

7. Even after they have been married for twenty years, his wife still frowns upon his habit of smoking in the study. （看不惯）

8. This Italian-made sweater is very expensive. But it doesn't look as good and comfortable as the sweater made in Hong Kong, which costs eighty dollars less. （还不如）

9. Edison （爱迪生） was a great American scientist. He invented a lot of things that are useful in our life. （发明）

10. At the airport, Mom said to him: "Call us as soon as you arrive at your university so that we won't worry." （省得）

八、读副课文：

（一）根据副课文判断正误：

1．"我"出差后，儿子来信，告诉"我"他结婚了。（ F ）

2．父母希望儿子结婚前，事先告诉他们，但他们也理解儿子的

作法。（ T ）

3．儿子是医生，儿媳是儿子大学的同学。（ F ）

4．父母为儿子结婚买了一套新家具。（ F ）

5．父母不关心儿子的婚姻，因为儿子有独立的思想。（ F ）

6．父母不干预孩子的婚事，让他们自己去决定自己的命运。（ T ）

（二）回答问题：

1．你认为儿子的作法对吗？

2．你同意那对父母对儿子婚姻的态度吗？

3．在你的国家或民族，人们结婚时一定要有仪式吗？什么样的仪式？

4．你的婚姻需要你的父母同意吗？

九、想一想，说一说：

1．你迷上过什么？

2．说一件好笑的事。

3．当你需要运动的时候，你选择什么方式？为什么？

4・1 我和老伴兒的拳舞之爭

一、寫出反義詞：

表揚---   早晨---

輕浮---   推辭---

聚---   吵---

二、作出動作，並寫出適當的動賓詞組：

例：舉---舉手

揮---   打---

扭---   跳---

拉---   推---

三、區分下列句子中 "一" 的不同意思，並模仿造句：

1・老伴兒天一亮就往公園跑。

2・打一早晨太極拳還不如我跳五分鐘的活動量大。

3・爺爺一喜歡就教她打几路拳。

四、仿照例句，用所給句式或詞完成句子：

（一）等......就......

例句：等雨停了，我們就去劃船。

1・_____。

2・_____。

141

（二）當．．．．．時，就．．．．．．

例句：<u>當</u>他拿到工資<u>時</u>，<u>就</u>馬上去買新衣服。

1．_____。

2．_____。

（三）對．．．．．．來說

例句：人口問題<u>對</u>很多國家<u>來說</u>，都是一大難題。

1．_____。

2．_____。

五、完成句子：

1．我們都想吃餃子，他則_____。

2．我喜歡唱歌，我妹妹則_____。

3．昨天他說想去中國，今天則_____。

4．我們坐飛機去旅行吧，省得_____。

5．你趕快復習功課吧，省得_____。

6．給你媽媽打個電話吧，省得_____。

7．這一百塊錢的衣服，還不如_____。

8．他不如他弟弟_____。

9．這里的天氣不如_____。

10．他既無錢，又無_____。

11．_____，可他還是去看電影了。

12．_____，但她還是覺得住在鄉下好。

六、造句：

1．跟不上

2．改行

3．歡迎＋N＋V

4．爭論

5．推辭

七、用所給詞語將下列句子譯成中文：

1. In recent years, the number of students applying to teachers' colleges has declined, largely because the profession of teaching is no longer attractive to young people. （近年來）

2. After being a truck driver for five years, he thought he needed to spend more time with his family. So he changed his profession and became a salesman. （改行）

3. Students from the Chinese Department performed a Chinese comedy at the New Year party. The funniest thing of all is that in the comedy, all the male students played the female roles , while all the female students played the male roles. （可笑）

4. The film is a truthful reflection of the suffering of the Chinese people during the Second World War. However, it might be too difficult for American students who have little knowledge of Chinese history. （對......來說）

5. To her surprise, Mrs. Li discovered that lately her son had become obsessed with *kung fu* movies and went to the movie theater after school every day. （迷上了）

6. This little boy told his grandma that after he grew up, he would make a lot of money and buy her a big mansion. The old woman was delighted with his childish promise. （等）

7. Even after they have been married for twenty years, his wife still frowns upon his habit of smoking in the study. （看不慣）

8. This Italian-made sweater is very expensive. But it doesn't look as good and comfortable as the sweater made in Hong Kong, which costs eighty dollars less. （還不如）

9. Edison （愛迪生） was a great American scientist. He invented a lot of things that are useful in our life. （發明）

10. At the airport, Mom said to him: "Call us as soon as you arrive at your university so that we won't worry." （省得）

八、讀副課文：

（一）根據副課文判斷正誤：

1· " 我 " 出差後，兒子來信，告訴 " 我 " 他結婚了。（ ）

2· 父母希望兒子結婚前，事先告訴他們，但他們也理解兒子的

　　作法。（ ）

3· 兒子是醫生，兒媳是兒子大學的同學。（ ）

4· 父母為兒子結婚買了一套新家具。（ ）

5· 父母不關心兒子的婚姻，因為兒子有獨立的思想。（ ）

6· 父母不干預孩子的婚事，讓他們自己去決定自己的命運。（ ）

(二) 回答問題：

1· 你認為兒子的作法對嗎？

2· 你同意那對父母對兒子婚姻的態度嗎？

3· 在你的國家或民族，人們結婚時一定要有儀式嗎？什麼樣的儀式？

4· 你的婚姻需要你的父母同意嗎？

九、想一想，說一說：

1· 你迷上過什麼？

2· 說一件好笑的事。

3· 當你需要運動的時候，你選擇什麼方式？為什麼？

4·2　　妻子下岗又上岗

一、填四字词组，用中文解释意思，并造句：

东____西____　　　恋恋_____　　　一塌_____

二、给句子中划线的词注音，并仿照例句造句：

1·妻子下了岗，我<u>倒</u>舒服了几天。

2·妻子下班<u>一</u>到家，常常就<u>倒</u>在沙发上睡着了。

3·妻子重新上岗后，第<u>一</u>天就上夜班。

4·妻子的下岗曾经给我们这个小家庭带来了<u>一</u>时的不安。

5·现在不行了，<u>得</u>早早起床，为自己和女儿准备早饭，忙<u>得</u>一塌
　　糊涂。

三、选词填空：

重新　　可口　　哪怕　　挺　　轻松

不如　　曾经　　坚持　　总

1·学校餐厅的饭不_____，我们_____去学校外面的饭馆吃饭。

2·_____作业再多，我也要按时完成。

3·这两天我_____忙的，没时间去看你。

4·他的作业写得很乱，老师让他_____做。

5·他_____学过中文，但是现在都忘了。

6·吃完饭，他_____不洗碗。

7·他生病了还_____来上课。

8·她每天只是看看书，散散步，生活很_____。

四、仿照例句，用所给句式或词造句：

（一）不......不行吗？

例句：你<u>不</u>开快车<u>不行吗</u>？

1·_____。

2·_____。

（二）哪怕......也得......

例句：<u>哪怕</u>明天下雨，我<u>也得</u>去跑步。

1·_____。

2·_____。

（三）怎么样，......

例句：<u>怎么样</u>，这次我的考试成绩又是全班最高的。

1·_____。

2·_____。

（四）......怎么办？

例句：我想去中国，可又没有钱，该<u>怎么办</u>？

1·_____。

2·_____。

五、造句：

1·尽管

2·不仅......连......

3．不管......（也）都......

4．如果......那么......

5．主动

6．趁

六、用所给词语将下列句子译成中文：

1. This morning, the secretary in our office suddenly announced that she will marry a French business man and will soon go to live with him in his country. （宣布）

2. She was very sad after her puppy died. Her husband said a lot of nice things to make her feel good. （安慰）

3. I am determined to join this group of tourists to go to Tibet this summer. I will make this trip even if I have to quit my job. （哪怕）

4. While your father is here, let's ask him to tell us about the terrible things that happened during the Cultural Revolution in China. （趁）

5. Despite the fact that you already have a college degree in computer science, to compete in the current job market, you have to take a couple of new courses in computers to update your knowledge. （尽管）

6. I didn't have breakfast this morning. I am so hungry that I must eat something immediately. （V+点儿什么）

7. I helped my friend to move into a new apartment yesterday. After we finished moving the last piece of furniture, I felt completely exhausted. （一塌糊涂）

8. There are only two days before the final examination. You must make the best use of your time to review all lessons covered during this semester. （抓紧时间+V）

9. When his wife told him that she spent two hundred and thirty-five dollars on this new toy, he became mad and wanted to return it to the toy store. However, after seeing his child like it so much, he changed his mind. （......成那个样子）

10. With the help of her friends and parents, she finally recovered from the devastating divorce, and decided to form a new family with a better man. （重新）

七、读副课文，回答问题：

1·妇女从家庭走向社会，标志着什么？

2·现在妇女又走回家庭的原因是什么？

3·现在的"专职家庭妇女"与以前的"家庭妇女"有什么不同？

4·如今妇女又走回厨房，你认为是社会的进步还是倒退？

八、想一想，说一说：

1·你认为妇女解放就是妇女一定要参加工作吗？

2·你认为什么是真正的妇女解放？在你的国家，妇女得到彻底地解放了吗？请举例说明。

4·2　妻子下崗又上崗

一、填四字詞組，用中文解釋意思，並造句：

東____西____　　　　戀戀_____　　　　一塌_____

二、給句子中劃線的詞注音，並仿照例句造句：

1·妻子下了崗，我<u>倒</u>舒服了幾天。

2·妻子下班<u>一</u>到家，常常就<u>倒</u>在沙發上睡著了。

3·妻子重新上崗後，第<u>一</u>天就上夜班。

4·妻子的下崗曾經給我們這個小家庭帶來了<u>一</u>時的不安。

5·現在不行了，<u>得</u>早早起床，為自己和女兒準備早飯，忙<u>得</u>一塌
　糊塗。

三、選詞填空：

重新　　　可口　　　哪怕　　　挺　　　輕鬆

不如　　　曾經　　　堅持　　　總

1·學校餐廳的飯不_____，我們_____去學校外面的飯館吃飯。

2·_____作業再多，我也要按時完成。

3·這兩天我_____忙的，沒時間去看你。

4·他的作業寫得很亂，老師讓他_____做。

5·他_____學過中文，但是現在都忘了。

6·吃完飯，他_____不洗碗。

7·他生病了還_____來上課。

8．她每天只是看看書，散散步，生活很_____。

四、仿照例句，用所給句式或詞造句：

（一）不……不行嗎？

例句：你不開快車不行嗎？

1．_____。

2．_____。

（二）哪怕……也得……

例句：哪怕明天下雨，我也得去跑步。

1．_____。

2．_____。

（三）怎麼樣，……

例句：怎麼樣，這次我的考試成績又是全班最高的。

1．_____。

2．_____。

（四）……怎麼辦？

例句：我想去中國，可又沒有錢，該怎麼辦？

1．_____。

2．_____。

五、造句：

1．盡管

2．不僅……連……

3．不管……（也）都……

4．如果……那麼……

5．主動

6．趁

六、用所給詞語將下列句子譯成中文：

1. This morning, the secretary in our office suddenly announced that she will marry a French business man and will soon go to live with him in his country.（宣布）

2. She was very sad after her puppy died. Her husband said a lot of nice things to make her feel good.（安慰）

3. I am determined to join this group of tourists to go to Tibet this summer. I will make this trip even if I have to quit my job.（哪怕）

4. While your father is here, let's ask him to tell us about the terrible things that happened during the Cultural Revolution in China.（趁）

153

5. Despite the fact that you already have a college degree in computer science, to compete in the current job market, you have to take a couple of new courses in computers to update your knowledge. （盡管）

6. I didn't have breakfast this morning. I am so hungry that I must eat something immediately. （V＋點兒什麼）

7. I helped my friend to move into a new apartment yesterday. After we finished moving the last piece of furniture, I felt completely exhausted. （一塌糊涂）

8. There are only two days before the final examination. You must make the best use of your time to review all lessons covered during this semester. （抓緊時間＋V）

9. When his wife told him that she spent two hundred and thirty-five dollars on this new toy, he became mad and wanted to return it to the toy store. However, after seeing his child like it so much, he changed his mind. （......成那個樣子）

10. With the help of her friends and parents, she finally recovered from the devastating divorce, and decided to form a new family with a better man. （重新）

七、讀副課文，回答問題：

1·婦女從家庭走向社會，標志著什麼？

2·現在婦女又走回家庭的原因是什麼？

3·現在的＂專職家庭婦女＂與以前的＂家庭婦女＂有什麼不同？

4·如今婦女又走回廚房，你認為是社會的進步還是倒退？

八、想一想，説一説：

1·你認為婦女解放就是婦女一定要參加工作嗎？

2·你認為什麼是真正的婦女解放？在你的國家，婦女得到徹底地解放了嗎？請舉例説明。

4·3　贝贝进行曲

一、给划线的词注音，解释其意思并造句：

1．朋友们都笑他<u>得</u>了"气管炎"。

2．儿子回答<u>得</u>脆响、特甜。

3．关键是他的营养<u>得</u>跟得上。

二、划线，组成动宾词组并解释意思：

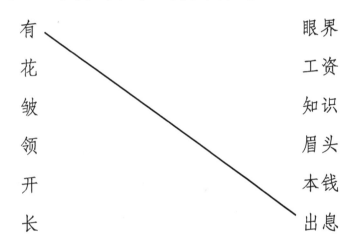

有　　　　　　　　　　眼界

花　　　　　　　　　　工资

皱　　　　　　　　　　知识

领　　　　　　　　　　眉头

开　　　　　　　　　　本钱

长　　　　　　　　　　出息

三、完成对话和句子：

1． A：＿＿＿＿＿＿＿＿＿＿＿＿＿＿＿＿＿＿＿＿＿。

　　 B：这倒是，你应该好好复习。

2． A：你要去中国工作，必须要学好中文。

　　 B：这倒是，＿＿＿＿＿＿＿＿＿＿＿＿＿＿＿＿＿。

3． A：下雨了，我们找个地方避避雨吧！

　　 B：反正＿＿＿＿＿＿＿＿＿＿＿＿＿＿＿＿＿＿＿。

4． A：你的父母不喜欢你的女朋友，怎么办？

　　　　B：反正＿＿＿＿＿＿＿＿＿＿＿＿＿＿＿＿＿＿＿＿＿＿＿＿＿。

5．要学好一门外语，关键＿＿＿＿＿＿＿＿＿＿＿＿＿＿＿＿＿＿＿＿。

6．减肥的关键是＿＿＿＿＿＿＿＿＿＿＿＿＿＿＿＿＿＿＿＿＿＿＿。

7．我们要去佛罗里达度假，一定要早订飞机票，到时候＿＿＿＿＿＿。

8．现在我讲关于明天考试的事，你要认真听，不要到时候＿＿＿＿＿。

四、仿照例句，用所给句式或词造句：

　　（一）一眼看上了……

　　例句：我一眼看上了那辆汽车，可是一看价格，我买不起。

1．＿＿＿＿＿＿＿＿＿＿＿＿＿＿＿＿＿＿＿＿＿＿＿＿＿＿＿＿＿。

2．＿＿＿＿＿＿＿＿＿＿＿＿＿＿＿＿＿＿＿＿＿＿＿＿＿＿＿＿＿。

　　（二）……没有关系，关键是……

　　例句：一个人聪明不聪明没有关系，关键是肯努力。

1．＿＿＿＿＿＿＿＿＿＿＿＿＿＿＿＿＿＿＿＿＿＿＿＿＿＿＿＿＿。

2．＿＿＿＿＿＿＿＿＿＿＿＿＿＿＿＿＿＿＿＿＿＿＿＿＿＿＿＿＿。

　　（三）连……也……

　　例句：他曾经学过两年法文，可是现在连一句法文也不会说了。

1．＿＿＿＿＿＿＿＿＿＿＿＿＿＿＿＿＿＿＿＿＿＿＿＿＿＿＿＿＿。

2．＿＿＿＿＿＿＿＿＿＿＿＿＿＿＿＿＿＿＿＿＿＿＿＿＿＿＿＿＿。

五、造句：

1．舍得（舍不得）

2．得意

3．伤心

4．迅速

六、填字组词，并解释意思，再选择其中的三个词，分别解
　　释下面的三幅画：

精____力____　　　　　　　____直____壮

无可_____　　　　　　　_____不下

（图1）

（图2）

（图3）

159

七、用所给词语将下列句子译成中文：

1. His research in the Library of Congress was very fruitful. Not only did he find all the documents that he needed, but he also discovered some useful materials that were not on his research list. （收获）

2. I am absolutely sure he is in his bedroom. As I passed by his door a moment ago, I heard him singing inside while listening to music. （一边......一边......）

3. He believes that if one wants to achieve success in this society, it doesn't matter if one is from a rich and powerful family. What really matters is that one should have a clear goal and work hard to achieve it. （关键）

4. After they both agreed to go to the concert rather than the movie theater, Mrs. Lin said to her husband: "Why don't we give the movie tickets to our neighbors? We are not going to see the movie anyway." （反正）

5. When he was a little boy, everyone who knew him said that this smart kid would have a promising future when he grew up. None of them expected that he would become a criminal at the age of 20. （有出息）

6. Seeing that everyone else at the meeting was in favor of the director's proposal, she reluctantly raised her hand to show that she, too, supported the director. （无可奈何）

7. Upon his return, he told his colleagues that the trip to Europe had greatly enlarged the scope of his vision. （大开眼界）

8. It rained for seven days. All the rice fields were flooded. Even the oldest man in the village had never seen such a terrible rain in his life. （连......也......）

9. After I woke up this morning, I turned on the radio and heard that the president resigned last night. （一 + V）

10. She begrudges every penny on her own food and clothes. However, when it comes to her son's education, she is willing to spend all the money she has saved. （舍不得，舍得）

八、读副课文：

（一）选择正确答案：

1·在这所小学，要上课时，为什么教室里还有很多家长？

     A：老师请家长帮忙

     B：父母要照顾孩子

     C：家长和孩子们一起上课

2·在上海的一所大学，什么事引起了人们的注意？

     A：上大学的人，家里都有汽车

     B：很多学生有私人汽车

     C：很多家长用汽车送孩子上学

3·家长来学校帮孩子做事，是因为：

     A：学生的生活能力不强

     B：孩子能照顾自己

     C：父母不愿孩子进入社会

（二）回答问题：

1·在上海大、中、小学里出现的这些现象说明了什么？

2·孩子的父母担心的是什么？而社会担心的又是什么？

九、想一想，说一说：

1·你认为贝贝的父母的想法、作法对吗？

2·在你的国家，父母怎样对待他们的孩子？

3·你认为正确的父母和孩子的关系是什么样的？

4·3　　貝貝進行曲

一、給劃線的詞注音，解釋其意思並造句：

1· 朋友們都笑他<u>得</u>了 " 氣管炎 " 。

2· 兒子回答<u>得</u>脆響、特甜。

3· 關鍵是他的營養<u>得</u>跟得上。

二、劃線，組成動賓詞組並解釋意思：

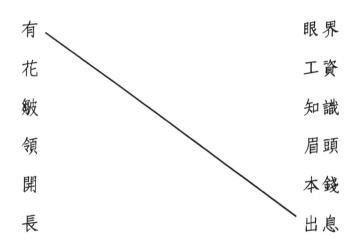

有　　　　　　　　　　眼界

花　　　　　　　　　　工資

皺　　　　　　　　　　知識

領　　　　　　　　　　眉頭

開　　　　　　　　　　本錢

長　　　　　　　　　　出息

三、完成對話和句子：

1· A：＿＿＿＿＿＿＿＿＿＿＿＿＿＿＿＿＿＿＿＿＿＿。

　　B：這倒是，你應該好好復習。

2· A：你要去中國工作，必須要學好中文。

　　B：這倒是，＿＿＿＿＿＿＿＿＿＿＿＿＿＿＿＿＿。

3· A：下雨了，我們找個地方避避雨吧！

　　B：反正＿＿＿＿＿＿＿＿＿＿＿＿＿＿＿＿＿＿＿。

4· A：你的父母不喜歡你的女朋友，怎麼辦？

B：反正_____。

5・要學好一門外語，關鍵_____。

6・減肥的關鍵是_____。

7・我們要去佛羅里達度假，一定要早訂飛機票，到時候_____。

8・現在我講關於明天考試的事，你要認真聽，不要到時候_____。

四、仿照例句，用所給句式或詞造句：

　　（一）一眼看上了......

　　例句：我一眼看上了那輛汽車，可是一看價格，我買不起。

1・_____。

2・_____。

　　（二）......沒有關系，關鍵是......

　　例句：一個人聰明不聰明沒有關系，關鍵是肯努力。

1・_____。

2・_____。

　　（三）連......也......

　　例句：他曾經學過兩年法文，可是現在連一句法文也不會説了。

1・_____。

2・_____。

五、造句：

1・舍得（舍不得）

2・得意

3・傷心

4・迅速

六、填字組詞，並解釋意思，再選擇其中的三個詞，分別解
　　釋下面的三幅畫：

精____力____　　　　　____直____壯

無可_____　　　　　_____不下

（圖1）

（圖2）

（圖3）

七、用所給詞語將下列句子譯成中文：

1. His research in the Library of Congress was very fruitful. Not only did he find all the documents that he needed, but he also discovered some useful materials that were not on his research list. （收獲）

2. I am absolutely sure he is in his bedroom. As I passed by his door a moment ago, I heard him singing inside while listening to music. （一邊......一邊......）

3. He believes that if one wants to achieve success in this society, it doesn't matter if one is from a rich and powerful family. What really matters is that one should have a clear goal and work hard to achieve it. （關鍵）

4. After they both agreed to go to the concert rather than the movie theater, Mrs. Lin said to her husband: "Why don't we give the movie tickets to our neighbors? We are not going to see the movie anyway." （反正）

5. When he was a little boy, everyone who knew him said that this smart kid would have a promising future when he grew up. None of them expected that he would become a criminal at the age of 20. （有出息）

6. Seeing that everyone else at the meeting was in favor of the director's proposal, she reluctantly raised her hand to show that she, too, supported the director. （無可奈何）

7. Upon his return, he told his colleagues that the trip to Europe had greatly enlarged the scope of his vision. （大開眼界）

8. It rained for seven days. All the rice fields were flooded. Even the oldest man in the village had never seen such a terrible rain in his life. （連......也......）

9. After I woke up this morning, I turned on the radio and heard that the president resigned last night. （一 + V）

10. She begrudges every penny on her own food and clothes. However, when it comes to her son's education, she is willing to spend all the money she has saved. （舍不得，舍得）

八、讀副課文：

（一）選擇正確答案：

1．在這所小學，要上課時，為什麼教室里還有很多家長？

　　　A：老師請家長幫忙

　　　B：父母要照顧孩子

　　　C：家長和孩子們一起上課

2．在上海的一所大學，什麼事引起了人們的注意？

　　　A：上大學的人，家里都有汽車

　　　B：很多學生有私人汽車

　　　C：很多家長用汽車送孩子上學

3．家長來學校幫孩子做事，是因為：

　　　A：學生的生活能力不強

　　　B：孩子能照顧自己

　　　C：父母不願孩子進入社會

（二）回答問題：

1．在上海大、中、小學里出現的這些現象說明了什麼？

2．孩子的父母擔心的是什麼？而社會擔心的又是什麼？

九、想一想，說一說：

1．你認為貝貝的父母的想法、作法對嗎？

2．在你的國家，父母怎樣對待他們的孩子？

3．你認為正確的父母和孩子的關糸是什麼樣的？

5 · 经济发展的动态

一、写出反义词：

城镇---   轻视---

失业---   提高---

二、用汉语解释下列的词：

前所未有   五花八门   养家活口

人力市场   固定工资   铁饭碗

中外合资   "万般皆下品，唯有读书高"

三、选词填空：

机会   固定   羡慕   改变

追求   开放   崇拜   终身

1·这里的桌椅是_____的，不能移动。

2·他有很好的工作，又有一个幸福的家庭，我很_____他。

3·那个科学家为世界作出了很大的贡献，我很_____他。

4·中国的改革_____，使人们有更多的_____学习外国先进的
   科学技术。

5·我离开家乡二十年了，当我再次回到那里时，看到它有很大
   的_____。

6·他为了_____自己的理想，离开了他的家乡。

7·他的爷爷_____生活在这个小城镇，从未去过别的地方。

四、仿照例句，用所给句式或词造句：

（一）．．．．．．以来，．．．．．．

例句：这是第二次世界大战<u>以来</u>，经济发展的最好时期。

1．_____。

2．_____。

（二）为．．．．．．提供．．．．．．

例句：学校<u>为</u>学生<u>提供</u>了良好的学习环境。

1．_____。

2．_____。

（三）不再．．．．．．

例句：他总骗人，我<u>不再</u>相信他说的话了。

1．_____。

2．_____。

五、造句：

1．一向

2．告别

3．习惯于

4．考虑

5．意味

6．不仅仅．．．．．．而是．．．．．．

六、用所给词语将下列句子译成中文：

1. As a military officer, the idea that a soldier must obey the order of his superior has been deeply rooted in his mind since his days in the navy academy. （扎根在）

2. During his childhood, he worshipped great scientists such as Newton （牛顿） and Einstein （爱因斯坦）. Every year, on the New Year's day, his first wish was always the same: go to the best college and become a scientist. （崇拜）

3. "I know why he has not agreed to a divorce." The woman was telling her friend about her boss. "He is afraid that people would look down upon him should he divorce." （让......看不起）

4. Before his death, the old farmer told his sons not to look down on farm work, and asked them to stay on the farm instead of going to work in the city. （轻视）

5. In the boy's mind, his father is not only an excellent basketball player but also the greatest hero in the whole world. （心目中）

6. In the past, college students in China liked to choose traditional disciplines (学科) such as mathematics and literature as their majors. Now more and more college students are inclined to major in practical disciplines such as computer science and business management. （倾向于）

7. He is used to reading the local newspaper before breakfast, and has not changed that habit since his marriage. （习惯于）

8. You should go shopping at the Commercial Street when you visit Tianjin. The stores there sell various kinds of goods. You can find anything you want there, from needles to cars. （五花八门）

9. The future career that my younger sister wants to pursue is to teach music in a kindergarten. （追求）

10. The hotel we stayed in for our summer vacation was very good. There was only one thing I was not happy with: it didn't provide breakfast for customers. （为......提供）

七、想一想，说一说：

1．你羡慕或崇拜什么人？

2．你看不起什么人？

3．你认为中国的经济发展为什么会带来这些变化？

4．没有"铁饭碗"是好事还是坏事？

八、写文章：

二十世纪九十年代以来，世界经济发生了很大的变化。在你的国家或地区，近十年来的经济发展给人民的生活和思想带来了什么变化？根据你的经历，写出其中主要的两个变化。

5· 經濟發展的動態

一、寫出反義詞：

城鎮---　　　　　　　　　　　　輕視---

失業---　　　　　　　　　　　　提高---

二、用漢語解釋下列的詞：

前所未有　　　　　五花八門　　　　　養家活口

人力市場　　　　　固定工資　　　　　鐵飯碗

中外合資　　　　　"萬般皆下品，唯有讀書高"

三、選詞填空：

機會　　　　　固定　　　　　羨慕　　　　　改變

追求　　　　　開放　　　　　崇拜　　　　　終身

1· 這里的桌椅是_____的，不能移動。

2· 他有很好的工作，又有一個幸福的家庭，我很_____他。

3· 那個科學家為世界作出了很大的貢獻，我很_____他。

4· 中國的改革_____，使人們有更多的_____學習外國先進的
　　科學技術。

5· 我離開家鄉二十年了，當我再次回到那里時，看到它有很大
　　的_____。

6· 他為了_____自己的理想，離開了他的家鄉。

7· 他的爺爺_____生活在這個小城鎮，從未去過別的地方。

四、仿照例句，用所給句式或詞造句：

（一）......以來，......

例句：這是第二次世界大戰<u>以來</u>，經濟發展的最好時期。

1. _____。

2. _____。

（二）為......提供......

例句：學校<u>為</u>學生<u>提供</u>了良好的學習環境。

1. _____。

2. _____。

（三）不再......

例句：他總騙人，我<u>不再</u>相信他說的話了。

1. _____。

2. _____。

五、造句：

1. 一向

2. 告別

3. 習慣於

4. 考慮

5. 意味

6. 不僅僅......而是......

六、用所給詞語將下列句子譯成中文：

1. As a military officer, the idea that a soldier must obey the order of his superior has been deeply rooted in his mind since his days in the navy academy. （扎根在）

2. During his childhood, he worshipped great scientists such as Newton （牛頓） and Einstein （愛因斯坦）. Every year, on the New Year's day, his first wish was always the same: go to the best college and become a scientist. （崇拜）

3. "I know why he has not agreed to a divorce." The woman was telling her friend about her boss. "He is afraid that people would look down upon him should he divorce." （讓......看不起）

4. Before his death, the old farmer told his sons not to look down on farm work, and asked them to stay on the farm instead of going to work in the city. （輕視）

5. In the boy's mind, his father is not only an excellent basketball player but also the greatest hero in the whole world. （心目中）

6. In the past, college students in China liked to choose traditional disciplines (學科) such as mathematics and literature as their majors. Now more and more college students are inclined to major in practical disciplines such as computer science and business management. (傾向於)

7. He is used to reading the local newspaper before breakfast, and has not changed that habit since his marriage. (習慣於)

8. You should go shopping at the Commercial Street when you visit Tianjin. The stores there sell various kinds of goods. You can find anything you want there, from needles to cars. (五花八門)

9. The future career that my younger sister wants to pursue is to teach music in a kindergarten. (追求)

10. The hotel we stayed in for our summer vacation was very good. There was only one thing I was not happy with: it didn't provide breakfast for customers. (為......提供)

七、想一想，説一説：

1 · 你羨慕或崇拜什麼人？

2 · 你看不起什麼人？

3 · 你認為中國的經濟發展為什麼會帶來這些變化？

4 · 沒有 "鐵飯碗" 是好事還是壞事？

八、寫文章：

　　二十世紀九十年代以來，世界經濟發生了很大的變化。在你的國家或地區，近十年來的經濟發展給人民的生活和思想帶來了什麼變化？根據你的經歷，寫出其中主要的兩個變化。

5·1　个人投资
买房子——新的领域

一、用汉语解释下列的词：

筹资　　　借款　　　积蓄　　　升值　　　社会热点

利润　　　探亲　　　业务　　　预付款　　寸土寸金

二、仿照例句，用所给句式或词完成句子：

（一）上＋N

例句：这个饭馆的菜很贵，每个菜都要上百元。

1·这里离他的家很远，_____。

2·除夕之夜，在纽约的时代广场，_____。

（二）一下子……

例句：有些人投资房地产，一下子就富起来了。

1·圣诞节之前，她为朋友们准备礼物，_____。

2·他很聪明，这么难的题目，_____。

（三）V＋起＋N＋来了

例句：他成立了一家公司，自己当起老板来了。

1·这几年，学电脑很热门，他辞掉工作，又回到大学，学_____。

2·他招收了几个学生，_____。

三、完成句子：

1·随着天气的变化，_____。

2·随着中国经济的发展，＿＿＿＿＿＿＿＿＿＿＿＿＿＿＿＿＿＿＿＿＿＿。

3·这个饭馆的菜这么贵，我们何不＿＿＿＿＿＿＿＿＿＿＿＿＿＿＿＿＿。

4·这里这么热，你何不＿＿＿＿＿＿＿＿＿＿＿＿＿＿＿＿＿＿＿＿。

5·你的钱包丢了，再找找，也许＿＿＿＿＿＿＿＿＿＿＿＿＿＿＿＿。

6·他今天没来上课，也许＿＿＿＿＿＿＿＿＿＿＿＿＿＿＿＿＿＿。

7·＿＿＿＿＿＿＿＿＿＿＿＿＿＿＿＿＿＿＿＿＿＿，打动了我的心。

8·＿＿＿＿＿＿＿＿＿＿＿＿＿＿＿＿＿＿＿＿＿，深深地打动了他。

四、造句：

1·直线上升

2·有的......有的......更有的......

3·惊讶

4·凭

5·具有

五、用所给词语改写句子：

（一）：就是......也......

　　1·即使你没有钱，我还可以让你吃饭。

　　2·如果他生病了，还要来上课。

（二）：将

　　1·明年我要毕业了。

　　2·他把我的书丢了。

（三）：于

1 · 我在2000年来到美国。

2 · 他把钱施舍给穷人。

六、用所给词语将下列句子译成中文：

1. The entire audience was deeply touched by the tragic life of the peasant girl in the Chinese movie *Yellow Earth*. Some of the viewers even wept. （打动）

2. He thought that his mother should not stay at home all the time. So he persuaded her to join the women's singing club in town. （说动）

3. I could not afford to buy this car. Even if I had money, I would not buy it because the color is ugly. （即使......也......）

4. He has apologized to you for his rude behavior. Why not give him another chance? （何不）

5. On what grounds do you draw that conclusion? （凭）

6. By means of his connections with government officials, the retired general helped to build a community library. （凭）

7. He volunteered to send the medicine to the patient's house, because he was familiar with the area where the patient lived. （对......熟悉）

8. Along with the development of social and economic systems, more and more people in China come to recognize the importance of laws. （随着......发展）

9. Ten years ago in China, if you wanted to make money quickly, you would have invested in real estate. However, it is no longer the case now. （投资于）

10. The rise of town-and-village enterprises （乡镇企业）, which occurred in the early 1980s, has exerted a great impact on Chinese economic reform. （兴起）

七、读副课文：

（一）回答问题：

1．房地产市场指的是什么？

2．在中国，"买卖土地"的意义是什么？有什么法律规定？

（二）用汉语解释下列句子：

1．向社会征聘有理想，踏实，努力，具有大专以上学历人才。

2．英语流利、积极进取、具有广州市区常住户口者。

3．一经录用，享受中外合资企业待遇。

4．人情所托，概不录用。

5．谢绝来访来电。

八、想一想，说一说：

1．你认为投资房地产这种发财的手段可靠吗？

2．你认为投资房地产成功的手段是什么？

5 · 1　個人投資
買房子 —— 新的領域

一、用漢語解釋下列的詞：

籌資　　　借款　　　積蓄　　　升值　　　社會熱點

利潤　　　探親　　　業務　　　預付款　　　寸土寸金

二、仿照例句，用所給句式或詞完成句子：

（一）上 +N

例句：這個飯館的菜很貴，每個菜都要<u>上</u>百元。

1 · 這里離他的家很遠，_____。

2 · 除夕之夜，在紐約的時代廣場，_____。

（二）一下子......

例句：有些人投資房地產，<u>一下子</u>就富起來了。

1 · 聖誕節之前，她為朋友們準備禮物，_____。

2 · 他很聰明，這麼難的題目，_____。

（三）V+ 起 +N+ 來了

例句：他成立了一家公司，自己當<u>起</u>老板<u>來了</u>。

1 · 這幾年，學電腦很熱門，他辭掉工作，又回到大學，學_____。

2 · 他招收了几個學生，_____。

三、完成句子：

1 · 隨著天氣的變化，_____。

2·隨著中國經濟的發展，＿＿＿＿＿＿＿＿＿＿＿＿＿＿＿＿＿＿＿。

3·這個飯館的菜這麼貴，我們何不＿＿＿＿＿＿＿＿＿＿＿＿＿。

4·這里這麼熱，你何不＿＿＿＿＿＿＿＿＿＿＿＿＿＿＿＿。

5·你的錢包丟了，再找找，也許＿＿＿＿＿＿＿＿＿＿＿＿＿。

6·他今天沒來上課，也許＿＿＿＿＿＿＿＿＿＿＿＿＿＿＿。

7·＿＿＿＿＿＿＿＿＿＿＿＿＿＿＿＿＿＿＿，打動了我的心。

8·＿＿＿＿＿＿＿＿＿＿＿＿＿＿＿＿＿，深深地打動了他。

四、造句：

1·直線上升

2·有的......有的......更有的......

3·驚訝

4·憑

5·具有

五、用所給詞語改寫句子：

（一）：就是......也......

　　　1·即使你沒有錢，我還可以讓你吃飯。

　　　2·如果他生病了，還要來上課。

（二）：將

　　　1·明年我要畢業了。

　　　2·他把我的書丟了。

（三）：於

1・我在2000年來到美國。

2・他把錢施舍給窮人。

六、用所給詞語將下列句子譯成中文：

1. The entire audience was deeply touched by the tragic life of the peasant girl in the Chinese movie *Yellow Earth*. Some of the viewers even wept. （打動）

2. He thought that his mother should not stay at home all the time. So he persuaded her to join the women's singing club in town. （說動）

3. I could not afford to buy this car. Even if I had money, I would not buy it because the color is ugly. （即使......也......）

4. He has apologized to you for his rude behavior. Why not give him another chance? （何不）

5. On what grounds do you draw that conclusion? （憑）

6. By means of his connections with government officials, the retired general helped to build a community library. （憑）

7. He volunteered to send the medicine to the patient's house, because he was familiar with the area where the patient lived. （對......熟悉）

8. Along with the development of social and economic systems, more and more people in China come to recognize the importance of laws. （隨著......發展）

9. Ten years ago in China, if you wanted to make money quickly, you would have invested in real estate. However, it is no longer the case now. （投資於）

10. The rise of town-and-village enterprises （鄉鎮企業）, which occurred in the early 1980s, has exerted a great impact on Chinese economic reform. （興起）

七、讀副課文：

（一）回答問題：

1. 房地產市場指的是什麼？

2. 在中國，"買賣土地"的意義是什麼？有什麼法律規定？

（二）用漢語解釋下列句子：

1. 向社會征聘有理想，踏實，努力，具有大專以上學歷人才。

2. 英語流利、積極進取、具有廣州市區常住戶口者。

3. 一經錄用，享受中外合資企業待遇。

4. 人情所托，概不錄用。

5. 謝絕來訪來電。

八、想一想，説一説：

1. 你認為投資房地產這種發財的手段可靠嗎？

2. 你認為投資房地產成功的手段是什麼？

5·2　　企业破产在中国

一、写出反义词：

直接---　　　　　　　　　　　结束---

亏损---　　　　　　　　　　　合法---

同意---　　　　　　　　　　　债务人---

二、用线连接有关的词：

　　　　　　　　　　　　　　　生产

法院————————————判决

银行　　　　　　　　　　　　　抵押

工厂　　　　　　　　　　　　　审理

商店　　　　　　　　　　　　　交易

　　　　　　　　　　　　　　　贷款

三、选词填空：

管理	审理	破产	产品
经营	权益	保护	合法
申请	提出	宣布	拍卖
设备	该	偿还	

这家企业_____很乱，_____一直亏损，负债率很高。_____

卖不出去。在这种情况下，他们只好向法院_____破产_____。

法院_____了这个案子。_____这家企业_____。并_____了

191

_____企业的生产_____。以此来_____债务。这样做，_____
了债权人和债务人的_____经济_____。

四、完成句子：

1．我忘了给我的花浇水，_____。（救活无望）

2．在今年的国际商品交易会上，_____。（成交额）

3．我们的婚姻法要_____。（保护）

4．我不能去参加那个晚会，_____。（得到......同意）

5．_____，不知为什么今天他迟到了。（一向）

6．中国实行改革开放的政策以后，_____。（逐步）

五、仿照例句，用所给句式或词造句：

（一）关于+N

例句：关于怎样投资的问题，我们还要考虑。

1．_____。

2．_____。

（二）跟......有关

例句：随着中国经济的发展，一些跟经济有关的法律还必须
修改，使其完善。

1．_____。

2．_____。

（三）为

例句：七月九日为这个工厂的建厂日。

1. _____。

2. _____。

　　（四）在＋N＋下

　　例句：<u>在</u>老师的帮助<u>下</u>，学生顺利地完成了这项实验。

1. _____。

2. _____。

六、造句：

1・按照

2・直接

3・整理

4・逐步

5・过程

6・改进

七、用所给词语将下列句子译成中文：

1. He usually doesn't like to borrow money. Now, he has no choice but to borrow money from his friends, because he is out of work and his wife is sick.（一向）

2. Although this new production plan sounds very good, it still has a lot of room for improvement.（改进）

3. As far as your father's opinion is concerned, you'd better take it into serious consideration, for you will have to get his permission first. （关于）

4. After talking with several students who lived in the same dorm, Professor Wang found that Miss Li's frequent absence from class had to do with some family problems. （跟......有关）

5. Thanks to the attractive environment for investment, over the past ten years, many new factories have been built in this coastal city. Among them are several joint-ventures. （其中）

6. Under the circumstances of insufficient supply of production materials, the newly-built mill plant has to be closed. （在......情况下）

7. According to the professor's requirements, students must turn in the final paper three days before the final exam week. Otherwise, the paper won't be accepted. （按照）

8. After several students reported that their bikes had been stolen, the school police began to investigate the situation. （对......进行＋V）

9. At the same time as he was seeking a job in the post office, he also sent applications to some graduate schools, hoping to continue his education on a higher level. （在......的同时）

10. Although China's legal system still has many problems, it is being perfected gradually. （完善）

八、读副课文，回答问题：

1·小李是从哪里来的？她羡慕什么？

2·她到城市后，觉得最大的问题是什么？她有什么新的打算？

3·六年后，小李的愿望实现了吗？她还想当文化人吗？

4·这篇课文说明了什么？

九、想一想，说一说：

1·中国实行破产法，对中国的经济发展有什么影响？

2·你能举出一个曾在世界上很有影响的公司依照破产法宣布破产的

例子吗？

5·2　　企業破產在中國

一、寫出反義詞：

直接---　　　　　　　　　　　　結束---

虧損---　　　　　　　　　　　　合法---

同意---　　　　　　　　　　　　債務人---

二、用線連接有關的詞：

生產

法院 ——————————————————— 判決

銀行　　　　　　　　　　　　　　抵押

工廠　　　　　　　　　　　　　　審理

商店　　　　　　　　　　　　　　交易

貸款

三、選詞填空：

管理	審理	破產	產品
經營	權益	保護	合法
申請	提出	宣布	拍賣
設備	該	償還	

這家企業_____很亂，_____一直虧損，負債率很高。_____賣不出去。在這種情況下，他們只好向法院_____破產_____。法院_____了這個案子。_____這家企業_____。並_____了

_____企業的生產_____。以此來_____債務。這樣做，_____
了債權人和債務人的_____經濟_____。

四、完成句子：

1·我忘了給我的花澆水，_____。（救活無望）

2·在今年的國際商品交易會上，_____。（成交額）

3·我們的婚姻法要_____。（保護）

4·我不能去參加那個晚會，_____。（得到......同意）

5·_____，不知為什麼今天他遲到了。（一向）

6·中國實行改革開放的政策以后，_____。（逐步）

五、仿照例句，用所給句式或詞造句：

（一）關於 +N

例句：關於怎樣投資的問題，我們還要考慮。

1·_____。

2·_____。

（二）跟......有關

例句：隨著中國經濟的發展，一些跟經濟有關的法律還必須
修改，使其完善。

1·_____。

2·_____。

（三）為

例句：七月九日為這個工廠的建廠日。

1 ． _____ 。

2 ． _____ 。

（四）在＋N＋下

例句：<u>在</u>老師的幫助<u>下</u>，學生順利地完成了這項實驗。

1 ． _____ 。

2 ． _____ 。

六、造句：

1 ． 按照

2 ． 直接

3 ． 整理

4 ． 逐步

5 ． 過程

6 ． 改進

七、用所給詞語將下列句子譯成中文：

1. He usually doesn't like to borrow money. Now, he has no choice but to borrow money from his friends, because he is out of work and his wife is sick. （一向）

2. Although this new production plan sounds very good, it still has a lot of room for improvement. （改進）

198

3. As far as your father's opinion is concerned, you'd better take it into serious consideration, for you will have to get his permission first. （關於）

4. After talking with several students who lived in the same dorm, Professor Wang found that Miss Li's frequent absence from class had to do with some family problems. （跟......有關）

5. Thanks to the attractive environment for investment, over the past ten years, many new factories have been built in this coastal city. Among them are several joint-ventures. （其中）

6. Under the circumstances of insufficient supply of production materials, the newly-built mill plant has to be closed. （在......情況下）

7. According to the professor's requirements, students must turn in the final paper three days before the final exam week. Otherwise, the paper won't be accepted. （按照）

8. After several students reported that their bikes had been stolen, the school police began to investigate the situation. （對......進行＋V）

9. At the same time as he was seeking a job in the post office, he also sent applications to some graduate schools, hoping to continue his education on a higher level. （在......的同時）

10. Although China's legal system still has many problems, it is being perfected gradually. （完善）

八、讀副課文，回答問題：

1・小李是從哪里來的？她羨慕什麼？

2・她到城市後，覺得最大的問題是什麼？她有什麼新的打算？

3・六年後，小李的願望實現了嗎？她還想當文化人嗎？

4・這篇課文說明了什麼？

九、想一想，說一說：

1・中國實行破產法，對中國的經濟發展有什麼影響？

2・你能舉出一個曾在世界上很有影響的公司依照破產法宣布破產的

例子嗎？

5·3   都市消费面面观

一、用中文解释下列词语的意思：

取而代之   丰富多彩   与此同时

热门话题   随之出现   亲朋好友

二、选词填空：

丰富多彩   与此同时   感觉到   反映

亲朋好友   原来   感兴趣   例外

1· 所有＿＿＿＿＿＿＿＿＿＿＿＿＿＿＿＿＿＿＿都参加了她的婚礼。

2· 这个暑假我为自己安排了＿＿＿＿＿＿＿＿＿＿＿＿＿的活动。

3· 他得到了一笔奖学金，＿＿＿＿＿＿＿＿＿他也收到了一家大公
   司的录用通知书，他不知道该怎么办。

4· 我对中国的京剧＿＿＿＿＿＿＿＿＿，所以以后我要研究京剧。

5· 我＿＿＿＿＿＿＿＿＿＿＿＿＿＿＿＿跑步是最好的锻炼方式。

6· ＿＿＿＿＿＿＿＿＿＿我住在印第安那州，现在我搬到了加州。

7· 他每天都去健身中心，刮风下雨也不＿＿＿＿＿＿＿＿＿＿。

8· 近几年来，中国快餐业的发展，＿＿＿＿＿＿＿＿＿人们的生活
   节奏加快了。

三、仿照例句，用所给的词改写句子：

例：老师表扬了小王。

→小王受到（了）老师的表扬。

1．战争威胁着这个国家。

2．人们伤害了许多动物。

3．政府限制人民的自由。

4．他爸爸批评了他。

5．西方思想影响了现代中国文化。

6．公司老板很重视他的建议。

四、用所给词语完成句子：

1． A：现在人们成天谈论的都是什么网上购物、网上投资。

B：＿＿＿＿＿＿＿＿＿＿＿＿＿＿＿＿＿＿＿＿＿＿。（热门）

2． A：你看我买的这件衣服怎么样？

B：＿＿＿＿＿＿＿＿＿＿＿＿＿＿＿＿＿＿＿＿＿＿。（得体）

3． A：现在已进入了信息时代，人们的通讯联络太方便了。

B：＿＿＿＿＿＿＿＿＿＿＿＿＿＿＿＿＿＿＿＿＿＿。（的确）

4． A：为什么在美国人们骑自行车都要戴头盔？

B：＿＿＿＿＿＿＿＿＿＿＿＿＿＿＿＿＿＿＿＿＿＿。（避免）

5． A：什么是你理想的生活方式？

B：＿＿＿＿＿＿＿＿＿＿＿＿＿＿＿＿＿＿＿＿＿＿。（追求）

6． A：我每天都要收到一大堆商业广告。

B：＿＿＿＿＿＿＿＿＿＿＿＿＿＿＿＿＿＿＿＿＿＿。（促使）

五、造句：

1·既......又......

2·即使......也......

3·不是......而是......

4·的确

5·逐渐

6·隔

六、读短文，做练习：

　　中国菜风味独特，风靡世界，吸引着世界各地的美食家。中国厨师在烹调时，善于利用各种天然调味品，做出甜、酸、苦、辣、鲜的味道来。人们在吃了中国菜以后，会情不自禁地说："味道太好了！"

　　中国菜油多、糖多、味道重、热量大，因此有些人在吃中国菜时担心会影响健康。其实，这种担心是不必要的。

　　据说，曾有人做过调查：发现中国人要比美国人多吃百分之二十的热量，但胖子却比美国少百分之二十五。这是不是完全和吃中国菜有关，还不能肯定，但可以说，中国菜能在全世界受到广泛欢迎，决不仅仅是因为"味道好"，它对人的身体健康也有好处。

　　（一）根据该短文的内容，选择下列词语的正确解释：

1·风味独特

　　A：风的味道很独特　　　　　B：很有特色

　　C：风吹来的味道很特别　　　D：有风的独特味道

2．风靡世界

    A：风吹遍了世界　　　　　　B：风把世界上的草吹倒了

    C：风把中国菜的味道吹遍世界　D：在世界上很流行

3．美食家

    A：美国的对食物有研究的人　B：美丽的对吃有研究的人

    C：对吃有研究的人　　　　　D：研究食物的专家

4．善于

    A：对人很友好　　　　　　　B：熟悉各种情况

    C：很善良　　　　　　　　　D：在某方面具有特长

5．天然

    A：来自天上的　　　　　　　B：自然存在的

    C：每天一样的　　　　　　　D：天空一样颜色的

6．情不自禁

    A：忍不住自己的感情　　　　B：自言自语

    C：不情愿　　　　　　　　　D：心情不好

（二）根据该短文的内容，回答问题：

1．中国厨师在烹调中国菜时有什么特点？

2．中国菜有什么特点？

3．有些人在吃中国菜时担心什么？

4．中国菜在世界上受欢迎仅仅是因为味道好吗？

5．为什么人们可以放心地去吃中国菜？

七、用所给词语将下列句子译成中文：

1. When evaluating a candidate for this position, you should pay attention to at least these four aspects: work experience, education, motivation, and personality. （方面）

2. Many American movie viewers feel that recent Chinese films are primarily characterized by a sad ending. （特色）

3. The farmers' market in my hometown has a rich array of farm produce. As long as you have money, you can buy whatever you want to eat. （丰富多彩）

4. To prevent students from wasting printer paper, the computer lab allows each student to print out only one copy of a document. （避免）

5. As the computer is playing a more and more important role in our lives, many people believe that traditional post offices will be soon replaced by e-mail. （取而代之）

6. Many people still remember the terrible life during the last economic crisis. That is why the news of another economic crisis impelled them to work harder, but spend less money than before. （促使）

7. Besides three required courses, a freshmen student can also choose to take a class he or she likes. （在......之外）

8. As the result of the one-child policy as well as the development of the economy, a family in China now can afford to spend much more money on the education of the child than before. （在......之上）

9. Because the new economic policy was sharply criticized by the majority of people in the country, the government decided to stop implementing it. （受）

10. Within two years, he turned a poorly-managed restaurant into a profitable business. Even those who had doubted his ability now agreed that he was indeed an excellent business manager. （的确）

八、读副课文，回答问题：

1·为什么"洋快餐"几乎垄断了北京的快餐业？

2·上海"荣华鸡"用什么方法跟"肯德鸡"竞争市场？结果如何？

3·"肯德鸡"对"荣华鸡"与其竞争怎么看？

4·你认为"荣华鸡"与"肯德鸡"的竞争说明了什么？

九、想一想，说一说：

1·你有什么样的消费观？

2·谈谈你的休闲活动。

3·谈谈经济发展与人民消费之间的关系？

5·3　都市消費面面觀

一、用中文解釋下列詞語的意思：

取而代之	豐富多彩	與此同時
熱門話題	隨之出現	親朋好友

二、選詞填空：

豐富多彩	與此同時	感覺到	反映
親朋好友	原來	感興趣	例外

1·所有_____都參加了她的婚禮。

2·這個暑假我為自己安排了_____的活動。

3·他得到了一筆獎學金，_____他也收到了一家大公司的錄用通知書，他不知道該怎麼辦。

4·我對中國的京劇_____，所以以后我要研究京劇。

5·我_____跑步是最好的鍛煉方式。

6·_____我住在印第安那州，現在我搬到了加州。

7·他每天都去健身中心，刮風下雨也不_____。

8·近幾年來，中國快餐業的發展，_____人們的生活節奏加快了。

三、仿照例句，用所給的詞改寫句子：

例：老師表揚了小王。

→小王受到（了）老師的表揚。

1· 戰爭威脅著這個國家。

2· 人們傷害了許多動物。

3· 政府限制人民的自由。

4· 他爸爸批評了他。

5· 西方思想影響了現代中國文化。

6· 公司老板很重視他的建議。

四、用所給詞語完成句子：

1· A：現在人們成天談論的都是什麼網上購物、網上投資。

B：＿＿＿＿＿＿＿＿＿＿＿＿＿＿＿＿＿＿＿＿＿。（熱門）

2· A：你看我買的這件衣服怎麼樣？

B：＿＿＿＿＿＿＿＿＿＿＿＿＿＿＿＿＿＿＿＿＿。（得體）

3· A：現在已進入了信息時代，人們的通訊聯絡太方便了。

B：＿＿＿＿＿＿＿＿＿＿＿＿＿＿＿＿＿＿＿＿＿。（的確）

4· A：為什麼在美國人們騎自行車都要戴頭盔？

B：＿＿＿＿＿＿＿＿＿＿＿＿＿＿＿＿＿＿＿＿＿。（避免）

5· A：什麼是你理想的生活方式？

B：＿＿＿＿＿＿＿＿＿＿＿＿＿＿＿＿＿＿＿＿＿。（追求）

6· A：我每天都要收到一大堆商業廣告。

B：＿＿＿＿＿＿＿＿＿＿＿＿＿＿＿＿＿＿＿＿＿。（促使）

五、造句：

1．既……又……

2．即使……也……

3．不是……而是……

4．的確

5．逐漸

6．隔

六、讀短文，做練習：

　　中國菜風味獨特，風靡世界，吸引著世界各地的美食家。中國廚師在烹調時，善于利用各種天然調味品，做出甜、酸、苦、辣、鮮的味道來。人們在吃了中國菜以后，會情不自禁地說：“味道太好了！”

　　中國菜油多、糖多、味道重、熱量大，因此有些人在吃中國菜時擔心會影響健康。其實，這種擔心是不必要的。

　　據說，曾有人做過調查：發現中國人要比美國人多吃百分之二十的熱量，但胖子卻比美國少百分之二十五。這是不是完全和吃中國菜有關，還不能肯定，但可以說，中國菜能在全世界受到廣泛歡迎，決不僅僅是因為“味道好”，它對人的身體健康也有好處。

　　（一）根據該短文的內容，選擇下列詞語的正確解釋：

1．風味獨特

　　A：風的味道很獨特　　　　　B：很有特色

　　C：風吹來的味道很特別　　　D：有風的獨特味道

2．風靡世界

    A：風吹遍了世界 　　　　　B：風把世界上的草吹倒了

    C：風把中國菜的味道吹遍世界　D：在世界上很流行

3．美食家

    A：美國的對食物有研究的人　B：美麗的對吃有研究的人

    C：對吃有研究的人 　　　　D：研究食物的專家

4．善于

    A：對人很友好 　　　　　　B：熟悉各種情況

    C：很善良 　　　　　　　　D：在某方面具有特長

5．天然

    A：來自天上的 　　　　　　B：自然存在的

    C：每天一樣的 　　　　　　D：天空一樣顏色的

6．情不自禁

    A：忍不住自己的感情　　　　B：自言自語

    C：不情願 　　　　　　　　D：心情不好

（二）根據該短文的內容，回答問題：

1．中國廚師在烹調中國菜時有什麼特點？

2．中國菜有什麼特點？

3．有些人在吃中國菜時擔心什麼？

4．中國菜在世界上受歡迎僅僅是因為味道好嗎？

5．為什麼人們可以放心地去吃中國菜？

七、用所給詞語將下列句子譯成中文：

1. When evaluating a candidate for this position, you should pay attention to at least these four aspects: work experience, education, motivation, and personality. （方面）

2. Many American movie viewers feel that recent Chinese films are primarily characterized by a sad ending. （特色）

3. The farmers' market in my hometown has a rich array of farm produce. As long as you have money, you can buy whatever you want to eat. （豐富多彩）

4. To prevent students from wasting printer paper, the computer lab allows each student to print out only one copy of a document. （避免）

5. As the computer is playing a more and more important role in our lives, many people believe that traditional post offices will be soon replaced by e-mail. （取而代之）

6. Many people still remember the terrible life during the last economic crisis. That is why the news of another economic crisis impelled them to work harder, but spend less money than before. （促使）

7. Besides three required courses, a freshmen student can also choose to take a class he or she likes. （在......之外）

8. As the result of the one-child policy as well as the development of the economy, a family in China now can afford to spend much more money on the education of the child than before. （在......之上）

9. Because the new economic policy was sharply criticized by the majority of people in the country, the government decided to stop implementing it. （受）

10. Within two years, he turned a poorly-managed restaurant into a profitable business. Even those who had doubted his ability now agreed that he was indeed an excellent business manager. （的確）

八、讀副課文，回答問題：

1．為什麼＂洋快餐＂幾乎壟斷了北京的快餐業？

2．上海＂榮華雞＂用什麼方法跟＂肯德雞＂競爭市場？結果如何？

3．＂肯德雞＂對＂榮華雞＂與其競爭怎麼看？

4．你認為＂榮華雞＂與＂肯德雞＂的競爭說明了什麼？

九、想一想，說一說：

1．你有什麼樣的消費觀？

2．談談你的休閑活動。

3．談談經濟發展與人民消費之間的關系？

AGMV Marquis

MEMBER OF SCABRINI MEDIA

Quebec, Canada
2001